BECOMING EINSTEIN'S TEACHER

*Awakening the **Genius** in Your Students*

ERIKA TWANI

Becoming Einstein's Teacher: Awakening the Genius in Your Students

For information about this title or to order other books and/or electronic media, contact the publisher:

Relational Learning, Inc.
www.ErikaTwani.com
et@erikatwani.com

ISBN:
978-1-7361683-2-5 (hardcover)
978-1-7361683-0-1 (softcover)
978-1-7361683-1-8 (eBook)

Printed in the United States of America

Cover and Interior design: 1106 Design
Editor: Rochelle Broder-Singer
Cover Photography: Yuganov Konstantin

To all learners.
There is hope to a better world, and it is in your hands.

To my late friend and source of wisdom, Greg Butler.
You would have loved the stuff in this book.

To my best friend and husband Brian,
with whom life is the perfect adventure.

TABLE OF CONTENTS

FOREWORD

"**It was the best of times, it was the worst of times . . .**" This famous opening line of Charles Dickens' *A Tale of Two Cities*, published in 1859, is a paradox we continue to live through. It describes life itself. Erika Twani pushes our thinking as she explores this paradox in this decade. It is the best of times, as signified by the remarkable technological developments that have enriched our lives in ways we never imagined, and will continue to do so for years to come. It can also be the worst of times if we freeze in the face of these advances in technology and ignore the message to evolve our children's education.

Like many teachers, my aspiration has always been to contribute to my students' success and happiness by helping them do what they love. I would have loved to be Albert Einstein's teacher. What could better describe my impact and influence on the world than to be the teacher of someone who has made such a significant contribution to our understanding of how the forces of the world work? I would also have loved to be Wolfgang Amadeus Mozart's teacher. Although such geniuses may be rare, after over 30 years of teaching people of all ages, I have come to appreciate the many scientists, artists, and others who, through our learning relationship, have found the genius within themselves. Erika's work is definitively a complementary addition to my work with personalized learning and Habits of Mind.

As you read this book, you will understand what teaching is essential to equip the 21st-century learner. Erika helps us understand the history of the development of artificial intelligence and the many ways that it is already in our lives—for better or for worse. She helps us observe the balance between artificial intelligence and biological intelligence, which we rarely discuss in the education world.

With great clarity, Erika provides an easily understood description about how the brain works and shows the relationship between what artificial intelligence can do and what biological intelligence can do, as well as how one enhances the other. As I read this book, I was constantly reflecting on the paradox that technology can be a source of destruction and fear or it can be a source of empowerment to construct a more thoughtful future. I, with Erika, choose the latter, and the rest of this book provides the stepping stones for that path.

Through her many practical examples, Erika asks readers to challenge themselves to take action to create a human-centered environment in which students are deeply committed and engaged in their experiences as learners. She shows us why learners need control over their choices, and why they must discover and aim to realize their dreams and aspirations in a clear and practical way. They need to recognize that knowledge is only "potential power." It becomes "power" to learners when it has a purpose with a definite end for its applicability.

In doing so, Erika provides insight into what it means to be a teacher in the 21st century. Understanding Erika's approach and putting it into practice may be a challenging task for those who have been teaching for many years. Yet, she manages to simplify a deep and complex methodology that honors the 21st-century learner's need for relationships, agency, and engagement. She reminds us that the teacher's role is that of a coach, providing continuous feedback and encouragement to persist.

~Dr. Bena Kallick

INTRODUCTION

"If not us, who? If not now, when?"

It was 2 a.m. on a weekday. I was on my 12th cup of coffee of the day, working on COBOL code after studying the basics of relational databases using a textbook borrowed from the library. For those unfamiliar with COBOL, it was a mainframe language used extensively during the last century. Yes, that old. I had to code on paper and then perforate various cards the size of a lottery slip. The next day, I would take the cards to the mainframe lab to process and hope it worked.

At 2 a.m., the household was silent. I could hear one or two cars passing by on the main road and crickets singing in dissonance. My body wanted to sleep so badly, like any human being. Coffee was my friend to help me stay awake every night. The days started at 6 a.m. and went through 3 a.m. the next day so I could work, attend college, and do my homework. I was on my fourth semester of a software engineering degree. I asked myself numerous times whether I should continue or drop out.

After a sip of my cold coffee that night, I started throwing up nonstop. First came whatever food I had the day before. Later came just the digestive juices the stomach releases when there is food to process. But there was nothing to process. I felt like my body was trying to purge all the caffeine left in it, almost trying to pump it from my bloodstream, with no success. I ended up at the ER and stayed there for the entire following day. After various rounds of IV fluids, the doctor released me only after I promised not to touch coffee any time soon.

I kept the promise. I didn't touch coffee again for 10 years. But I still had to stay awake until 3 a.m. every day. So I switched to black tea, Coca-Cola, and guarana—a fruit from the Amazon full of caffeine—and continued my journey to graduate from college while working. I do not recommend you try these drinks or any other stimulants at all! I would organize my life completely differently today in order to fulfill all the demands of life and still be healthy.

This experience helps me relate to how young adults are coping with college and the pressure to succeed, given the continuous competitiveness in modern society. You should watch the 2018 documentary *Take Your Pills* by director Alison Klayman. It shares the rough reality of students and young professionals today. I wonder if I would be taking those pills, swallowing them with Red Bull, if I were in college today.

Life was miserable during my college time. High levels of stress were normal: bills to pay, courses to excel at, work to deliver, clients to smile at, hours of packed buses to ride, dark streets to cross late at night, and so on. I had plenty to worry about: Would I have any money left to eat? Would the bus be late? Would someone attack me on the dark streets? Would that customer buy? Would I survive this nightmare? Would life continue to be this tough? My family always told me that the only way out of poverty was to study—and study hard.

Poverty is humiliating. It creates a continuous fear of failure, a sensation of doubt that the strategy for escaping it will work. But, since it was my only option, I learned to suck it up, to go through the system, to play the game, to do whatever teachers asked me to do and move on with honors ahead of others. After all, I was taught over and over that just a few chosen people will get to the highest level in life, so my grades had to be better than others'.

I entered each semester ready to push myself really hard to get to the end of the tunnel as quickly as possible, where light had to definitively be brighter than the current darkness. The best part of college was the great friends I made for life. I witnessed them go through the same difficulties I went through. I am sure most of you will relate to this story. The vast majority of the population in the world comes from humble and stressful beginnings. I am almost positive you also heard that you must study hard, that school is the only way to be successful in life, and thus, took a similar route through the education system.

Things used to be different, though. I had a blast until eighth grade. I learned to read and do math at the age of six, got assessed at school, and got "promoted" to third grade at the age of seven. I was really scared of those big nine-year-old kids and couldn't stop crying, so the school downgraded me to second grade, but definitively not first grade. School was fun and I was interested in learning. I read many books, played sports, played an instrument in the school band, and was a reporter for the school's monthly newspaper. I used to learn math so fast that my math teacher would entertain me with the next grade's subjects to keep me busy and make sure I left the other kids alone.

Other children found a reason to bully me at that time: my big ears. They called me Dumbo. I justified the extra-size ears as a personal advantage that helped me play the guitar and the piano without reading music. Yes, I could play even classical music by ear, but I mostly played pop. I told the kids I had very accurate hearing, but, between you and me, the real reason was my inability to read music.

Then, somehow, everything changed in high school. It was all about testing, all about getting into college. It was a flood of subjects I would never use in my life—lots of nonsense. At the end of my senior year in high school, we had to be able to regurgitate everything we, in theory, learned during our entire lives up to that point. It was the beginning of the pain of college: the fight to get a piece of paper, a certificate that proved our teachers were satisfied with our answers on exams.

Those years of high school and the following five years of college were the most challenging years of my life as a student. It was so painful that I promised myself to never touch a book again after graduating from college. My brain fought really hard to make sense of memorizing these subjects, so misaligned with my interests, and to justify going through that while I could be doing something more productive with my life!

In the end it paid off, but I really wish it had been less painful. After college, I had my own IT company, sold my shares to my business partners, then worked for large tech corporations—Oracle and Microsoft, steadily moving on the path toward becoming a higher-level, worldwide executive VP of some sort. I had a blast working for those organizations. I met so many people, interacted with customers from different countries, traveled around the world representing these big names in the tech industry, earned an MBA, and made friends for life. I broke my promise and started reading books again. I made peace with the school mayhem, although I do not wish this experience on my worst enemy.

~ A NEW PERSPECTIVE ON EDUCATION ~

In 2007, I was promoted to lead a new Microsoft venture: to shape the company's products, services, and business model for underserved communities. I was particularly focused on the education industry, traveling to different countries to learn from the best pedagogical practices schools were using and exploring how technology would enhance them and scale them.

Microsoft sponsored many pilot projects to explore how the best pedagogic models would improve and/or scale using technology. As you can imagine, once the source of financing was gone, so was that project. Pilot projects in most schools never became sustainable, but one did—a project at a public rural school in Colombia.

I visited that school many times and witnessed the transformation: Students were confident, followed their dreams, and never used a lack of resources or their financial limitations as excuses. They learned all these life principles in school. I looked at them and saw joy for being there. These children were happy, regardless of their circumstances. I thought to myself, These students are geniuses! This generation pursues their dreams with joy. They clearly understand the outside will never fulfill them as individuals, but what they have inside will. These students found the genius they have within. And because of that, they did pretty well academically.

In that same school, I met Andres, who touched my heart in such a way that I could not stop crying after a 20-minute conversation with him. We were in his classroom and I was kneeling next to him. He talked about his life journey and I listened, while looking at him in disbelief. I am even crying as I write these words. After that chat, I had to leave the room. I was filled with turmoil, from my brain to my stomach. I sobbed for who knows how many hours. People were trying to calm me down. I couldn't explain my tears, as the pain in my heart was so big. I thought to myself, How could I be so egoistic? I felt I was self-centered in my success, protective of MY career, MY family, MY friends, my this, and my that, while these educators were fostering human achievement.

Not for a moment did I think I could be a teacher. I was very happy to have chosen my career because it prepared me for that moment. Education had a whole new meaning for me suddenly! It was no longer a means to an end, but something that could create real readiness for life—a journey during which, with the support of teachers, we can clearly define our dreams, select and build our own pathways, and choose how to feel at each step along the way. I came to understand that genius is not necessarily related to science. In the case of these students, it was related to their ability to discover their passions and work on developing them, coached by their teachers.

The difference between these students' experiences and mine is simple: Their dreams were aligned to their learning and actions. They were intrinsically motivated, rather than extrinsically motivated like I was. Destiny is not set in stone, and these students' circumstances were not a limitation on realizing their potential. They moved from meritocracy to life purpose, without changing their circumstances. Me? I had no joy as a student. I was just trying to live my life as "they" told me to. In fact, more than 55% of students who had experiences like mine have dropped out of school. Meritocracy excludes whomever is unable to adapt to its rules.

~ RELATIONAL LEARNING AND FINDING NEW MEANING IN MY LIFE ~

How many people do you know who would love to pursue their dreams but restrain themselves because it is "too late" or who have no idea where to start? What if we had learned, in the safety of the school environment, to make decisions, make mistakes, and correct ourselves while coached by teachers? What if we could experience continuous joy along the way, because somehow, even as children, we knew we were set to be whomever we wanted to be?

Those were the questions I started asking myself while deep diving into Relational Learning, the framework we used at that rural school in Colombia. Relational Learning fosters the coconstruction of knowledge and practices that helps everyone's potential flourish. It nurtures a profound respect for each member of the learning community, in which each person is unique and highly complex, is in permanent development, is the author of their own life, and is an active actor in society. I learned about this framework with its mastermind, Julio Fontan.

Relational Learning is not a new concept. It dates back at least 40 years. It incorporates the best of personalized learning, project-based learning, competency-based learning, and autonomous learning. What is new in this book is that I share a clear process to make Relational Learning efficient, effective, and scalable. It enables students to learn anything they want while practicing effective learning habits. For teachers, it is like being with your students 24x7, whenever they want to learn, because of the skills you help them develop.

What if we could scale Relational Learning from one public school to millions? How many children would have the same opportunity to realize their potential and be happy? What difference would it make in the world? You may argue that this is a nice dream, but that it is impossible to make it a reality in the public school system. Oh, the changes that would be required in public policy, school settings, curriculum, resources, and so on!

Indeed, the latest pedagogy models and learning methodologies all preach that we must change something. Some schools have ventured into making those changes, but the vast majority has not and will not. Human beings simply do not like change. Therefore, if we depend on change for anything significant to happen in education, we may be waiting forever.

While I was on this quest to understand education, four friends died within the span of one year. Three were in their early 50s, one of them was 40. I attended two of the services and witnessed how friends and family remembered their lives: happy moments, legacy, teachings, and marks. I thought to myself, If I died today, what would people talk about in my eulogy? In my dying moment, would I trade one day of the safety of my comfort zone for the chance of living my unrealized dreams? I must decide what my legacy will be right now, because the world needs me. This is the time to bring forth what I have inside!

That experience with Andres and the death of my friends changed the trajectory of my entire career and life. Sipping a latte (no pure coffee for me, thank you!) with Julio one day, we reflected on the famous saying: If not now, when? If not us, who? Although my high-paying job provided a great deal of security, I was ready to change my life. I quit my job in 2011 and founded Learning One to One Foundation with Julio. Somehow, by that point, the decision was a no-brainer and life had an entirely new meaning. It felt like this is what I was preparing to do my whole life.

We invited experts in pedagogy, psychology, and philosophy to join our research and development team and scale Relational Learning to the world. We established three core principles:

1. Most importantly, build from where school systems are, from the practices of leaders and teachers. Coconstruct knowledge and practices, just as Relational Learning works with students.

2. Never stop researching and developing. After all, the human mind is continuously growing, and we must shape education to foster its evolution.

3. Empower educators to continue investing in research and development in their areas of greatest abilities.

Relational Learning asks for no change, only for the deepest desire to enable students to learn, which is our starting point. We combined decades of effective pedagogy practices with the engineering discipline of building trustable and efficient processes and procedures to scale. To date, we have served tens of thousands of students in various countries, enabling the broader school community to have the same experience as the first school we worked with, through continuous professional development for the education community.

~ ENABLING TEACHERS TO USE RELATIONAL LEARNING ~

We saw it was possible to scale Relational Learning regardless of community contexts: rural or urban, virtual or homeschooling, with or without technology, few or abundant resources, this or that curriculum, low or high income. Relational Learning starts from the core of each teacher and student. Within one year of implementing our Relational Learning Framework, these schools showed an average of 40% improvement in reading comprehension, 37% of students finishing one full grade in seven months or less, 100% curriculum coverage, and dropout rates close to zero.

Now we want you to have access to Relational Learning, and this book is the first step to make it happen. The second step is yours, when you read the book and start using the framework presented here. In this book, I share not a theory or an experiment, but the practical work my organization does in partnership with schools and school systems around the world. This framework does not require a revolution in education systems; instead, it guides the community on simple practices that will benefit them academically and in life.

The principles presented here are simple but transformative. Stop reading right now if you are already committed to taking no action. Otherwise, open your mind to this journey of discovery of humanity's infinite capacity to create and recreate the world around us through a personalized learning experience that fosters continuous skill development and autonomy. Then, use the simple practices provided in this book and witness the transformation.

Although our primary focus is an education context, you can use the Relational Learning Framework at work and in your own life. You will notice I use "learners" more often than "students," to denote that we are all lifelong learners. You will also notice we aim to develop human potential, regardless of a person's socioeconomic or heritage background. We do not intend to change people's natures, but, rather, to improve the learning processes, enable learning, and light up their creative capacities.

My tech job is long gone. Andres, his classmates, and his teachers gave me a new life perspective and inspired me to do things differently. I now have a mission instead of a job: to enable human achievement at its highest level and unlock human potential, starting at school. In the same way children must learn to walk and talk, they must learn to use their minds to their fullest.

This book is for raving enthusiasts of a better world. Now it is your turn to join a community of thousands of teachers already reporting unimaginable results with their students. We are in this together, to bring forth the genius within each human.

CHAPTER 1

WAS EINSTEIN STUPID?

"There is no passion to be found playing small, in settling for a life that is less than the one you are capable of living."

–Nelson Mandela

It was the year 1881, in the city of Munich, Germany. The family had just moved there from Ulm for a business opportunity Mr. Hermann Einstein was pursuing with his brother Jakob. The beautiful suburban house they moved into had a spacious garden where children would play for hours. Little Albert Einstein was 2 years old and could barely speak. It worried his mother, Pauline Koch, to the point that she took him to a doctor, only to learn there was no specific diagnosis for his lack of speech. The child was healthy, just delayed in speaking.

Albert Einstein would learn words and keep repeating them over and over again. Members of his family labeled him "almost backwards." On the other hand, because of his slow development, he learned to observe the world around him in much more detail than a "normal" child, a skill that would help him in his quest to discover how the universe works.

Little Einstein was prone to temper tantrums, perhaps because they allowed him to express himself while his speech was limited. In today's world, a modern psychologist might diagnose him with a developmental disorder.[1] Among other characteristics, he was, from a young age, nonconformist; he also had no filters, lacked empathy, was a loner (he did not enjoy mingling with other children), and tended to disrespect authority figures. How many of those have you had in your classroom? Or, if that describes you, do not worry: That is your genius within.

Einstein was 5 years old and sick in bed when his father gave him a compass. That day his condition appeared to get worse—not due to his sickness, but because he was feverishly excited to learn about the invisible force field that attracts a compass needle toward the north. That device ignited in him a passion for discovering hidden fields and their governance in nature.

By the time he was 6, Einstein's parents enrolled him at a local Catholic school. His favorite subject was religion, and he had a strong interest in math. His personality continued to characterize him, to the point that one of his teachers said he "would never amount to much." He was the perfect example of how a distracted child behaves. Other children bullied Einstein because he was a Jew. Fights and insults often occurred during his walks to and from school. The most significant impact of bullying in his childhood was his growing feeling of being an outlier, which he would carry throughout his life.

As the years passed, Einstein became extraordinarily good in math, learning much by himself. By the age of 15, he mastered differential and integral calculus, while failing in anything related to language. Words were not his thing; they didn't belong in the "interesting" category by his measures. Einstein hated high school because of the imposed learning-by-repetition and teachers' dislike of students asking questions. Teachers were the authority and the source of knowledge, and students had to respect them as such. Prussia's worship of military structure profoundly influenced the school's dynamics, which emphasized a mechanical discipline comparable to the march of soldiers on the streets of Munich.

If you perceive any similarities between young Einstein's experience and our current public education system, you are entirely right. Horace Mann, an American education reformer and promoter of public education, visited various European schools in 1843, among them the ones in Prussia. At that time, Prussia was the economic power of the 19th century and carried significant political influence. As the secretary of the Massachusetts Board of Education (the first of its kind in the U.S.) and a national advocate of access to education, Mann proposed to adopt the Prussian model of public education.

Horace Mann's vision for the public education system was to improve humankind, to be inclusive of all children regardless of their backgrounds, to be nonsectarian, to have a standardized teacher-training system, and, most of all, to teach children within the tenets of a free society. Those were noble principles, different from the real dictatorial Prussia's principles of education. Perhaps Mann was unaware of those differences.

The perception many of us have that something is wrong with our current education system is the same sentiment Einstein had when he was in high school. The remarkable Dr. Carl Sagan also noticed a fundamental issue with the U.S. system:

> *"You go talk to kindergarteners or first-grade kids, and you find a class full of science enthusiasts. They ask deep questions! 'What is a dream?' 'Why do we have toes?' 'Why is the moon round?' 'What is the birthday of the world?' 'Why is the grass green?' These are profound, important questions, and just bubble right out of them!*

> *You go talk to 12th-grade students, and there is none of that. They become latent and incurious. Something terrible has happened between kindergarten and 12th grade, and it is not just puberty."*[2]

Ask yourself: Would this brain numbness occur if we had the right education system?

Dr. Laurence Steinberg, a professor at Temple University in Philadelphia, surveyed 20,000 U.S. high school students about their motivation and engagement in school. One-third of the students said they get through the school day by engaging in an idle pastime with their friends while neglecting schoolwork. Almost 90% said they had copied homework from a friend in the prior year. Fewer than 20% think it is essential to do well in school. In his book, *Beyond the Classroom*, Steinberg argued that the "problems in students' attitudes, values, and beliefs about the importance of education underlie the current crisis in American education."[3]

~ TAPPING INTO CHILDREN'S INTRINSIC CURIOSITY AND DESIRE FOR EXPLORATION ~

Children were designed for success and engineered for accomplishment. Curiosity and exploration are an unconditioned stimulus for younger children, and learning is an unconditioned response. Their brains' reward system is wired to reward them for exploring their interests and finding answers to their questions. The world is theirs to conquer! Would a toddler ever learn to walk if she were afraid to fall? However, soon after a child enters the school system, the brain's natural curiosity stops being rewarded. They start living for the expectations of others and pursuing empty objectives. Their minds become conditioned to seek the approval of others and to worry about their circle's opinions. They are unmotivated to explore anything outside the ordinary. The natural connection between curiosity, exploration, and rewarded learning is broken.

Today's children live in a duality: On one hand, they have the innate capacity to think for themselves. On the other hand, they are conditioned to seek validation. This duality kills children's potential and, I believe, contributes to rising suicide rates among teenagers. In the U.S., suicide was the second-leading cause of death among people aged 15 to 24 in 2017, according to the National Center for Health Statistics and the Centers for Disease Control and Prevention. Among people aged 15 to 19, there were 47% more suicides in 2017 than in 2000.[4]

School children are dying each day, whether physically or mentally. The emotional scars caused by the lack of excitement in everyday education can kill their potential to lead an outstanding life. How do we stop this loss of potential? How do we tap into children's innate ability to learn—and to do so independently?

Einstein was passionate about learning, and I genuinely believe all students are just like him. He wanted to learn so badly, but was so unhappy with his high school experience that he became depressed. His teachers almost campaigned for the boy to leave school. Einstein's depression evolved into a nervous breakdown after the business his father and uncle started went bankrupt and the family began to drown in debt.

Ultimately, the family had to move to northern Italy, leaving Einstein behind to finish school. Some months later, Einstein decided to drop out of school and joined his father and uncle in rebuilding their business. To Einstein, it was not a big deal—he disliked school, anyway.

Despite dropping out of school, Einstein continued to learn. Perhaps the difference between the usual student who drops out of school and Einstein is that Einstein had already established an intrinsic motivation for learning about one aspect of science when his father gave him that compass. He named his passion "invisible fields." Because of that intrinsic motivation, he had the grit to continue his studies. Regardless of the circumstances, he would likely have found a way. The vast majority of us, though, rely only on an extrinsic motivation for learning—one that forces us to go through the system just because it is the "right thing to do" according to the society we live in. My extrinsic motivation was to get out of poverty. If all children have a sense of wonder—an intrinsic motivation—inside of them, why do we have an education system designed around extrinsic motivation, rather than drawing out their natural curiosity, creativity, and passion?

So many school dropouts love learning and genuinely miss the real-life application of what they were learning. There was just no connection between their passion and what they were learning in school—that is the reason they became bored!

History has shown us that magic happens when intrinsic motivation is finally awakened. There are no limits to what humans can do. Sir Richard Branson, who has dyslexia, dropped out of school at the age of 16, founded Virgin Group, and became a multibillionaire. Thomas Edison, one of the world's greatest inventors, had only three months of schooling. Walt Disney dropped out at the age of 16. And so did Sir Elton John, Charles Dickinson, and Ray Kroc. Lady Gaga, a college dropout, has won more than 200 music awards. Surely there are successful people who went through school all the way to doctorate degrees. The question is: Did they do so because someone told them to or because they found a school that aligned their dreams with their learning?

When he left school, Einstein promised his parents he'd study by himself and be admitted to the Federal Polytechnic Institute in Zurich, Switzerland (today known as the Swiss Federal Institute of Technology Zurich). Indeed, the Poly's director allowed Einstein to apply for the entrance exam in October 1895, despite the fact that he was two years under the admission age of 18 and did not have the required high school certificate. On the exam, Einstein earned spectacular results in science and math, but failed miserably in all other subjects. The Poly's director rejected his application but advised Einstein to spend a year at the cantonal school, a locally run school, in a nearby village, attending a sort-of GED program (equivalent to a high school diploma) and prepare for the entrance exam in the following year. The cantonal school was Einstein's dream come true. Repetitions and memorizations were prohibited! Instead, children learned to think for themselves, to reach their conclusions, and to find answers their own way.

Einstein's sister, Maja, later described the cantonal school, which she also attended: "Pupils were treated individually. More emphasis was placed on independent thought than on punditry, and young people saw the teacher not as a figure of authority, but, alongside the student, a man of distinct personality." Einstein loved that school. In his words, "when compared to six years' schooling at a German authoritarian gymnasium, it made me clearly realize how much superior an education based on free action and personal responsibility is to one relying on outward authority."

It was in this school that Einstein developed the ability to translate complex science into simple examples ordinary people could understand. It started with riding a train along with a light beam. Then other images came along in his research: the trampoline, the elevator, the falling apple, and so on. In simple models lie the explanations of the universe.

The innovative Swiss system designed by Johann Heinrich Pestalozzi and used at the cantonal school eliminated illiteracy in the country by 1830.[5] Imagine if Horace Mann had gone to Switzerland in 1843 and promoted a public school system like the cantonal school that Einstein loved. The education system in the U.S. would be very different today. Perhaps Pestalozzi's death in 1827 prevented Horace Mann from becoming acquainted with the Swiss learning innovation, and to consider its replication in the U.S.

For Einstein the cantonal school was life-changing. With his learning finally tied to his passions, he eventually passed the Zurich Polytechnic entrance exam and enrolled in a four-year mathematics and physics program in 1896. He wanted to become a professor and continue his research on theoretical physics. He was blessed with an uncle who supported him financially during these four years.

Throughout his college time, Einstein was Einstein, engaging in disagreements with professors, rebelling against following orders, criticizing the evaluation system, questioning the status quo, and so on. He and his friends thought the college's lectures were out of date and studied more-recent theorists by themselves. I bet you can relate to that, and you are not alone. I had the same experience: I never used anything I learned from my college professors, but instead used what I learned at work.

Einstein used to skip boring classes, such as experimental and lab practices with Professor Jean Pernet. He would throw instruction sheets in the trash without even reading them, execute the experiment, get to the right answer, and deeply frustrate Pernet. Pernet asked an assistant once, "What do you make of Einstein? He always does something different from what I have ordered." The assistant replied, "He does indeed, Herr Professor, but his solutions are right, and the methods he uses are of great interest." Pernet gave Einstein the lowest grade possible (one out of six) and made history for failing a genius in his favorite subject: physics.

Einstein graduated in 1900, the first generation in his family to graduate from college. He was ranked fourth out of five, at the bottom of his class. This was not because of poor performance on his final exams, but because he did a lame job on his final paper. It was a subject picked by his dissertation advisor, not by him, and was unrelated to his passions. But he knew he had to complete it to graduate. This rebellion cost him various junior professor positions he applied for over the following two years. The references his college professors gave to potential employers were disappointing, perhaps something that might translate today into "great IQ (intellectual intelligence), but no EQ (emotional intelligence)."[6]

It was only in 1902, with the help of his college friend Marcel Grossmann, that Einstein got his first real job, at the Swiss Patent Office, where he worked for seven years before finally becoming a professor at the University of Bern.

Perhaps his lack of EQ helped Einstein's determination to prove someone else wrong, to get what he wanted for his life and not what someone else chose for him. Other brilliant minds have found the strength to persevere in pursuit of their dreams, and that is when great things happen. We would not have Harry Potter if J. K. Rowling believed she had to have a "safe" career to keep her financially stable and had no time to write. We would not have met the fastest man in a pool and most decorated Olympian of all time if Michael Phelps believed ADHD should prevent him from doing anything with excellence.

Fifteen years after his college graduation, Einstein published his greatest work of art, the general theory of relativity. It was the culmination of years of research in theoretical physics and the answer to so many questions about the universe. Einstein contributed to much more during his lifetime, including quantum mechanics and the understanding of how energy relates to mass through his famous equation $E=mc^2$.

Was Einstein stupid? Perhaps he heard someone call him such because of his late development and nonconformism, among other personal characteristics. History proved whoever called him that wrong. Einstein's story shows how much value an individual can bring to the world through the realization of their potential, especially when that individual's combination of skills makes them unique.

The children sitting in your classroom today will also bring great value to the world. They might need a little help to get started, and then they will do the rest.

CHAPTER 2

BEING A GENIUS

"Genius is 1% inspiration and 99% perspiration."

–THOMAS EDISON

When I met Andres at his school in rural Colombia, he was 17 years old. He looked like a sharp young man, well dressed and with neat hair. In that year, his fellow students elected him as their representative to the school's board of directors. He was hosting a youth radio program in town and set to receive a full scholarship to one of the top universities in the country. Looking at these accomplishments, you would conclude the boy was definitively a leader. But his story was very different from what you might think.

Although his future looked—and was—bright, Andres lived in a context of limited socioeconomic opportunities. He had lost his vision at the age of 13. He learned braille but, living in a rural community, his future was very limited. His mother wanted the best for him, regardless of the circumstances. She convinced the local school to accept Andres, after much resistance. So Andres attended a regular school, even though his condition did not allow him to learn as other children did. He went to school to prepare for the only destiny he was told to expect. Shame, stress, depression, and anxiety are familiar emotions for children living under these conditions.

At the time I met Andres, I was working at Microsoft. My job was to introduce technology and innovative learning systems around the world. My team and I were on a quest to find transformative learning systems whose effectiveness could be enhanced by technology. Our team in Colombia started working with Andres' school the year before my visit, implementing an autonomous learning model that fostered students' potential. The learning system, Relational Learning, was based on fostering student agency, or learning autonomy, by nurturing the development of intellectual, socioemotional, and personal skills while learning the required curriculum.

Once Andres understood the concept behind what the school was offering him through the Relational Learning Framework, he took full advantage of it as his only hope for a better future. Through Relational Learning, he learned to be independent, to respect others and himself, to have self-esteem, to argue effectively, and to discuss solutions with his classmates. Andres turned out to be a natural leader! With his teachers' guidance, he evolved into his natural role in this world, and other children eventually ignored his vision impairment. Instead, they focused on his contributions to the group and to the community. Andres had a dormant genius inside him, yearning to take action and lead. His genius was never bothered by his sight limitations. As soon as Andres' teachers helped him realize that, he became the leader he was meant to be from the day he was born.

- "GENIUS" THROUGH THE YEARS -

What does it mean to be a genius? The Merriam-Webster dictionary defines genius as "a single strongly marked capacity or aptitude" or "an exceptional intellectual or creative power or other natural ability." Thomas Edison supposedly quipped, "Genius is 1% inspiration and 99% perspiration." In truth, we are yet to have a scientific explanation for genius. The popular belief is that a genius is someone with exceptional original intellectual capacity or productivity in a specific area. Einstein reinforced this concept when the media shared his discoveries, explained through metaphors that anyone could grasp.

Ancient Romans believed genius was a creative spirit present in every individual, place, or thing—a sort of guardian angel who would accompany someone from birth to death. In truth, Romans needed an explanation for the events and accomplishments in someone's life. Horace (65 BC–8 BC), an eminent Roman lyric poet during the time of the emperor Octavian, explained genius as "the companion which controls the natal star; the god of human nature, in that he is mortal for each person, with a changing expression, white or black."[7] Horace described different geniuses, depending on the talent that a person exhibited: artist, fighter, philosopher, musician, speaker, and so on.

By the 18th century, the word "genius" evolved from describing an external entity into describing talents and inborn nature. Thus, the concept moved from "having a genius" to "being a genius." From then on, researchers undertook extensive studies to explain intelligence. English statistician Sir Francis Galton (1822–1911) pioneered the concept that intelligence is hereditary and that genius is rarely seen in the general population, as shared in his book *Hereditary Genius*, published in 1869.[8] This theory included the first attempt to create a standardized test to measure intelligence.

In 1905, French psychologists Alfred Binet (1857–1911) and Dr. Théodore Simon (1873–1961) created the Binet-Simon intelligence measurement scale, which became widely used.[9] In 1899, Binet had become a member of the Free Society for the Psychological Study of the Child, which was committed to using science to study children. Around this time, France passed a law to make schooling mandatory for children aged 6 to 14. The French government appointed Binet and other members of the society to the Commission for the Retarded (as it was called then), with the mission to answer the question: "What should be the test given to children thought to possibly have learning disabilities, that might place them in a special classroom?"

Binet believed in children's diverse intelligence, but the practical use of the Binet-Simon scale limited any ideas that deviated from the purpose the French government determined. The scale was mainly focused on verbal abilities and aimed to identify mental disabilities in schoolchildren. If identified as having disabilities, those children would be labeled "sick," and, therefore, told they should leave school. There is a chance Einstein would have been asked to leave school using this system!

The Binet-Simon scale became known in the U.S. after the American psychologist and eugenicist Dr. Henry H. Goddard (1866–1957) translated and published it in 1910. Goddard was an advocate of using intelligence tests in public institutions, including schools. As a eugenicist, he believed the genetic quality of the human race could improve by "excluding certain genetic groups judged to be inferior, and promotion [of] other genetic groups judged to be superior."[10]

American psychologist Dr. Lewis Terman (1877–1956), a Stanford University professor and also a eugenicist, believed that intelligence was inherited and was the strongest determinant of a child's future. He proposed adjustments to the famous test, resulting in the Stanford-Binet

Intelligence Scale, published in 1916. It became the most commonly used intelligence test in the U.S. for decades.

Terman called the highest score of this new scale "genius." He and his colleague Dr. Catharine Cox Miles (1890–1984) proceeded to perform a lifelong longitudinal study of Californian children called "Genetic Studies of Genius." Teachers recommended many students for the study, including two who were rejected because of their low scores on the Stanford-Binet scale.[11] The two later became Nobel Prize winners in physics: William Shockley (1956) and Luis Walter Alvarez (1968). Like these two, many other people have debunked the theory behind the need for a high IQ to succeed in life.

Cox Miles published books in which she concluded that being a genius requires traits beyond a high IQ. By 1937, she had dropped the use of the term "genius" for the highest classification of the Stanford-Binet. Dr. David Wechsler (1896–1981), a Romanian-American psychologist and author of well-known intelligence scales such as the Wechsler Intelligence Scale for Children, later concluded, "We are rather hesitant about calling a person a genius on the basis of a single intelligence test score."[12]

Since their initial development, intelligence scales have been used in ways their creators never intended. Binet had intended for his scale to be used to identify children's learning disabilities and areas in need of improvement. But the French government used it to identify the mentally disabled and invite them to leave the school system. In the U.S., Terman proposed using the Stanford-Binet scale to assign children to their appropriate job tracks. His studies served as the basis for creating the gifted programs used today in most U.S. schools.

Can you imagine having your child labeled as mentally disabled and invited to leave school? It happened to Thomas Edison and Albert Einstein, two students whose genius was misinterpreted.

~ THE GENIUS AS CREATIVE THINKER ~ THE PROBLEM-SOLVERS WE NEED TODAY

American Dr. George Land (1932–2016), a general systems scientist, dedicated his career to studying the enhancement of creative performance. This led to his Transformation Theory, which argues that natural processes integrate principles of creativity, growth, and change. More than 400 corporations worldwide license his unique processes for strategic thinking and innovation, which all start in people's brains.

Land identified two types of thinking processes related to creativity:

- **Convergent thinking**: in which ideas are judged, criticized, refined, combined, and improved at the conscious level; and

- **Divergent thinking**: in which new, original ideas are imagined, which often happens at the subconscious level.

In 1968, Land started a longitudinal research study on divergent thinking, or the capacity to explore different solutions; he designed his own categorizations of an individual's creative potential. He created a simple test to explore the many usages a person can give to an object. As adult "problem-solvers," we tend to feel we must have an immediate answer for everything. Most of the solutions we propose are related to what we already know. For example, if I ask you to think of ways to use a paper clip, you may answer: to hold two or more sheets together, and maybe to open the SIM card compartment of your mobile phone. Younger children will think of 30 more uses for the paper clip because they are not as limited by what they know from the past.

Land studied 1,600 children for 15 years. From ages 3 to 5, 98% of children scored within his "creative genius" category. Five years later, only

32% of the same children scored within the category. By the time they reached the age of 15, only 10% of children scored within the creative genius category. The same test applied to more than 200,000 people over the age of 25 found only 2% fell into this category.[13]

Like so many children and so few adults, Einstein always practiced divergent thinking, the trait of a genius. He once said, "If I had an hour to solve a problem, I'd spend 55 minutes thinking about the problem and 5 minutes thinking about solutions." And, he noted, "Imagination is more important than knowledge."

Why do so many adults seem to lose our divergent, or creative, thinking skills as we grow older? Land concluded that "noncreative behavior is learned" in schools because we teach children to use both convergent and divergent thinking processes at the same time. The brain can only process one kind of thinking at a time or it shuts down. In other words, children are born creative geniuses, but learn to suppress creative behavior in school. Their natural senses are numbed to fulfill a social norm of being educated in the way someone else has decided is most effective.

The solution, according to Land, is to allow students to use one thinking process at a time, to encourage imagination and new ideas, and to only then, allow students to consider which idea is useful for them.

So, if we use a new framework for teaching that allows students to exercise imagination—or divergent thinking—related to their passions, we can have brilliant, creative minds even once they leave school. This framework requires that we believe all children are born creative geniuses, regardless of their socioeconomic status, their place of birth, or their differences.

The word genius comes from Latin *genii*, which means "to produce, to create, to beget, to give birth to." Coincidence or not, the word education comes from Latin *educare*, meaning, "to bring forth from within." Both require action to give birth to what students have within. The genius is inside, and education brings it out! If genius is 1% talent and 99% work, we ought to help students develop working habits that get them to 100% genius.

This distinct approach to teaching children how to think is more important than it has ever been. The way we learned to solve problems in school—with heavy emphasis on what is already known—no longer works. The problems we face in the world are more threatening than ever before: wars, globalization, diseases, competition, hunger, poverty. Today, more than ever, we need geniuses.

Thankfully, we can make use of simple methodologies to engage the brain's creativity. We can use our creative minds to come up with extraordinary solutions to today's problems. We already have what it takes to create the future we want.

This is exactly what Andres' teachers believed. He could have been lost as a learner, blind and with limited tools to live an outstanding life. His teachers used a learning framework to help him discover his personal genius and make use of it. He learned tools for understanding the world around him and how to keep learning. This was no easy task for Andres or his teachers. To bring out a genius, a student must be humble, vulnerable, open to the possibilities ahead, determined, persistent, passionate, and resilient. Teachers are the support system for children to reveal their genius. Revealing a child's genius helps to give them a purpose and bring them into harmony with life.

~ ADDING EMOTIONAL INTELLIGENCE (EQ) TO THE PICTURE ~

Years after Cox Miles' and Wechsler's conclusions that genius is defined by traits besides a high IQ score, scientists were still challenged by the reality. Dr. Travis Bradberry, a dual PhD in clinical and industrial-organizational psychology, and Dr. Jean Greaves, a PhD in industrial-organizational psychology, wrote in *Emotional Intelligence 2.0*: "People with the highest levels of intelligence (IQ) outperform those with average IQs by just 20% of the time, while people with average IQs outperform those with high IQs 70% of the time." How could that possibly be? The answer was back in the 1800s.

When Phineas was born in 1823 in Lebanon, New Hampshire, his parents, Eaton and Hannah Gage, had no idea their son would have such an influence on our understanding about intelligence. Phineas P. Gage (1823–1860) was perfectly healthy, never had one day of sickness, and his shape as a young adult resembled that of a body builder, although there was no such a thing at that time. Phineas enchanted people around him with his refined social skills. Because of that, he ascended easily to become the boss of any crew he worked with in his field of construction. Although he never went to school, he displayed traits of a genius—particularly in his incredible skills building railroads.

At the end of the summer of 1848, Phineas and his crew were engaged in what was supposed to be just another easy day at work in Vermont. They were boring into an outcrop of rock using blasting powder, a fuse, and a vertical tamping iron that was almost 4 feet long and 1¼ inches in diameter. The tamping iron was used to direct the energy of the explosion into the rock. The powder exploded, rocketing the tamping iron straight through Phineas' left lower jaw, then his upper jaw, cheekbone, left eye, the left side of his brain, and the frontal bone of his skull. In the 19th century, the only safety gear workers wore were hats to protect them from the sun. As the tamping iron flew through his head, Phineas was propelled backward. The iron landed 80 feet away, Phineas convulsed for a few minutes, then he stood up and rode back to town.

Dr. Edward H. Williams and Dr. J. M. Harlow found Phineas sitting on a chair on the porch of his hotel. Phineas explained to the doctors how the accident happened and that he was bleeding and vomiting occasionally. Williams was in total disbelief that this 25-year-old man was even alive, let alone able to speak as if he had only pinched a finger. The doctors operated on him to put his broken bones back together. After the surgery, he had periodic convulsions and sometimes "lost control of his mind."[14] As the days passed, Phineas got worse, with prominent infection in his wounds. Everyone was waiting for his death, but Harlow was able to contain the infections.

Just 10 weeks after his surgery, Phineas was strong again and started improving bit by bit. He had lost his left eye, one tooth, and part of his brain's frontal lobe, and was left with scars. Although his body recovered well, people close to him found Phineas a completely different man after the accident. He became aggressive, profane, angry, impulsive, and easily lost track of work. As years passed, though, he became more "normal." Doctors concluded this was because the job he eventually got as a stagecoach driver required repeating the same thinking structure over and over again, which allowed him to form new neural connections and get into routines in which he controlled any impulsiveness he may have had. Within those routines, he was able to plan ahead and adapt to anything that might arise on the route.

Phineas became a required study case for neurologists, psychologists, and neuroscientists. How could someone survive such a trauma and still live even after losing part of the brain? What are the effects of brain damage on personal and social skills? Phineas' case was crucial for our understanding of the regulation of emotions in the brain: They are triggered in the limbic system, or midbrain. The prefrontal cortex then identifies the emotion and makes the final call as to how we react to it. Phineas lost part of his prefrontal cortex and, therefore, could not regulate his emotions. He was functioning on automatic mode. Study after study proved this supposition of how we process emotions to be right.

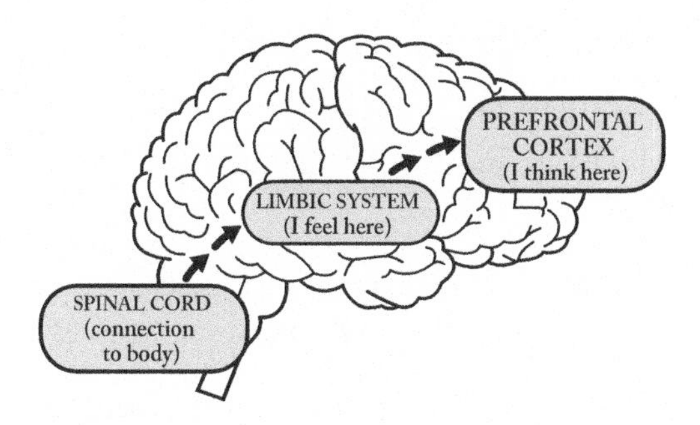

Figure 2.1: the brain's mechanics

The term "emotional intelligence" was first mentioned in 1964 by Dr. Joel Robert Davitz and Dr. Michael Beldoch,[15] clinical professors of psychology in psychiatry, both from Columbia University. In 1995, the concept gained exposure to the public in science journalist Dr. Daniel Goleman's book *Emotional Intelligence*. Goleman defined it as "how we handle ourselves and our relationships."[16]

Goleman laid out three facets of emotional intelligence, also known as EQ:

- **Self-awareness**: recognizing what and why we are feeling;
- **Self-management**: how we handle distress emotions, our ability to be attuned to emotions when needed, how we align our actions with our passion, and how we foster positive emotions; and
- **Empathy**: our ability to recognize others' emotions.

Scientists concluded that EQ is an important factor in someone reaching a higher position in an organization.[17] It is a skill that allows a person to manage others and coax them to give their best, to execute a strategy with excellence through a team. Goleman explained it in this way: Most engineers, PhDs, and high-performing professionals have a standard IQ deviation of 115 or higher. That means most of their peers also have IQs of 115 or higher. What sets apart an individual who becomes a leader is EQ.

Here is one example of the importance of EQ in leadership: Apple cofounder Steve Jobs imagined the iPhone. He specified what the device should be like to his engineers and set up a plan. But Jobs did not design the phone or build it. The engineers did. IQ helped Jobs come up with the idea for the product—a creative solution to a problem that deviated from what was standard, known, and expected at the time. It helped him foresee the opportunity and put a strategy in place to get the market to adopt his new product. EQ helped him to tell the iPhone's story, to motivate his team, to inspire the company and early buyers.

With this understanding, some schools have invested in developing children's EQ. Investments in professional development for teachers and new curriculum led to an average of 10% improvement in behavior, academic achievement, and social skills.[18]

Our understanding of the factors that predict success is no longer limited to those privileged to be born with a "high IQ." The combination of cognitive, personal, and socioemotional skills is the real predictor of success. When we are aware of our feelings, we can process any situation and use cognitive skills to take action. We are emotional beings and, therefore, must develop both cognitive and emotional skills to become outstanding humans.

The importance of EQ is underscored by a 2019 report by the Brookings Institute.[19] It predicts that artificial intelligence (AI) will continue to replace jobs that can be automated, usually low-paying, but which also include analytic-technical and professional jobs. In other words, AI will replace jobs that require repetition and those that are highly correlated to IQ. On the other hand, jobs that require interpersonal relationships, such as those in education, healthcare support, and personal care services, are likely to survive the advent of AI. These jobs are highly correlated to EQ.

In Colombia, Andres' teachers invested in increasing his EQ along with his IQ, nurturing and bringing out the genius leader that was always inside him. Because of this, he went on to graduate from college with a degree in communications and started working at the nation's Communications and Technology Ministry. There, he created a national program that allows blind and deaf people to attend the theater and understand movies using technology! Now imagine Andres' life without this school experience. What a waste of potential it would have been for himself and his country. Think of all the untapped potential out there, people who never had the same chance as Andres. Would we be in a better place as a society if these learners realized their potential? We have an urgent need to focus on *human development.*

By developing outstanding individuals—creative geniuses who realize their unique potential—we improve the whole community. In the 2008 article *Education and Economic Growth*, several academics shared an eye-opening microeconomic analysis that can be summarized like this: Improving the cognitive skills of each learner, rather than just ensuring school attainment, may enable a GDP increase of one full percentage point annually over a 40-year period.[20]

"I have no special talents. I am only passionately curious," Einstein said. Imagine if you had taught Einstein and were the young genius' memorable teacher. How would you feel? The fact is, now that you understand what genius is, you may realize geniuses are sitting in your classroom as you read these words, just waiting for you to help liberate their potential.

CHAPTER 3

THE PLIGHT OF A TEACHER

"Every child deserves a champion—an adult who will never give up on them, who understands the power of connection, and insists that they become the best they can possibly be."

-**Rita Pierson**

In the Oscar-winning movie *The Cider House Rules*, Dr. Wilbur Larch (Michael Caine) put the boys to bed at the St. Cloud's orphanage in rural Maine with a salute: "Good night, you Princes of Maine, you Kings of New England!" One boy asks, "Why does Dr. Larch say that every night?" "Dr. Larch loves us," answers a second boy. "But why does he do that?" insists the first boy. "He does it because we like it," replies another boy. "Do you like it, Curly?" challenges the first boy. "Yeah." "I like it too," says the first boy again.

The Cider House Rules is fiction, but it teaches us priceless real life lessons. The story will make the macho man's eyes water and the lighthearted cry convulsively. In this scene, Dr. Larch demonstrates how much he values the orphan boys through his good night salute, which the boys interpret as "love." Dr. Larch names the boys monarchs of the city and state they live in, with inherited sovereign rights to rule!

What the boys were unaware of is that they do, in fact, have the sovereign right to rule over their own lives, and so do you and I. We are all monarchs, with sovereignty over our life experience. We all have an innate potential to realize, regardless of the families we are born into, the countries we are born into, or our socioeconomic status. After all, the most important thing is not where we come from, but where we are heading. It is up to us to venture into growth or to remain in safety. No one can do this for us. There is a profound implication in the understanding that we are all monarchs: You respect yourself for your royalty, and you respect others because they are royals too.

Therefore, the next time you see your students, remember this: Each child is unique by design. There are no other fingerprints like theirs in the world, and there never will be. Each of their brains has 100 billion neurons, out of which you can guide them to shape (100 billion)^{n} combinations and form neural networks: knowledge, ideas, creations, concepts, and so on. These are all theirs and differ from those of any other human being that ever existed, exists, or will exist. These are your students' geniuses! What would the world be without each of them? Celebrate their existence and their potential!

Your students' bright future is only possible through learning, as learning shapes and brings forth their genius. The more they learn and experience with the right guidance, the wiser they will be. Therefore, never limit their learning, or you will be limiting their life experience.

Be grateful each day for the possibilities ahead for each child. The only way to have joy today is to love what they do today. Go out there and help your students live their lives fully.

However, I know this isn't easy. According to the Merriam-Webster dictionary, as a noun, "plight" means (1) a solemnly given pledge; and (2) an unfortunate, difficult, or precarious situation. Education truly is the plight of each teacher. On one hand, they pledge a commitment to foster human achievement. On the other hand, the challenges of their work are enormous in this journey to fulfill their pledge.

The teaching profession is one of the noblest, in my opinion. Teachers commit their professional lives to helping human development flourish. Yet, even a cursory look at the data shows how deeply teachers are challenged today:[21]

1. More than 200,000 teachers leave the profession each year, and two-thirds leave for reasons other than retirement;

2. 50% of teachers have considered quitting;

3. 58% of classroom teachers describe their mental health as "not good." They are in a classroom with your children right now; and

4. 72% of teachers report they have felt moderate to extreme pressure to improve their students' test scores, with the pressure coming from school boards and school administrations.

According to the Learning Policy Institute, which conducts and shares research related to education policy and practice, the exodus of new teachers after their first year of teaching can be cut by more than half through quality mentoring, effective integration of new teachers into the school culture, collaboration, and extra resources. Sadly, only 3% of teachers starting out get this kind of support.[21]

According to the National Center for Education Statistics (NCES), by year 2028, we will need 3.9 million teachers in the U.S. education system, a 7% increase from 2016.[22] At the same time, there is definite and logical pressure to move toward a more personalized learning model, in which each child receives the necessary attention to learn well. Under the current education framework, a more personalized model would require doubling the number of teachers in U.S. schools, bringing class sizes to approximately 10 or less students.

Such small classrooms would allow teachers to provide personalized attention to each student. Yet, how can we consider personalized learning when the number of talented teachers is declining and the ones that stay describe their mental health as "not good?" Moreover, how can teachers focus on personalizing students' learning experience if the system calls for better performance on standardized testing? It is really the plight of a teacher: the genuine desire to fulfill their professional pledge and the challenges of doing so within a 19th-century education model.

~ A FAMILIAR STORY—A TEACHER'S LIFE ~

I interviewed various teachers to explore their experiences first hand. Among many, this story shares some of the experiences that many teachers expressed. I want this teacher to tell her own story, so here she is, in her own voice:

> I am Chanel Williams, a high school teacher.
>
> When I was in elementary school, I used to play teacher with my brother. I enjoyed helping him learn. He had issues,

especially with reading. I asked him questions, helped him with homework, and inspired him. Well, the inspiration part was kind of tough; it mostly involved saying, "Don't run out! Don't quit on me!" I did believe my brother was smart. I cared and wanted him to succeed.

I came from humble beginnings, living in Hollywood, Florida, with my family. I went to public school. At school, no one ever recognized any particular passion in me. I was just another student going through the system, sitting in classes, doing what I was told to do. Eventually I enrolled in college to become a teacher.

When I started teaching, I rolled my sleeves up and prepared to work hard! I wanted to save the world, like most teachers. I started with this relentless passion to make a difference, and, teaching history, I was unstoppable for four straight years . . . until reality hit. That was 2008, when the recession changed my course. Significant budget cuts meant the only way for the administration to keep me in the system was to have me teach reading.

I accepted the challenge, believing I would have the required support from the administration and district, including materials and professional development. That was not the case. There was a lack of resources, which can significantly affect a child's education. Many of my high school students didn't know how to read. They endured lots of trauma and lived in poverty. I was left on my own—with only my imagination, will, and motivation—to teach these children.

I tried hard. But after four years of facing a lack of appreciation and resources, I gave up. I left the system, taking time off to soul-search. It was so hard. I felt terrible for my students. I realized I loved teaching and couldn't see myself doing anything else. Memories of teaching my brother came back to me and I really wanted to help other kids. How could I consider leaving this behind? So, I returned to my passion.

After six months away, I started working in a charter school, but that was worse than my previous experience! My work was unappreciated. I left the charter school to go back to a public school in Miami-Dade. This particular high school was taken over by the state because it had underperformed for so many years. The state was experimenting with a new concept, education transformation. I had excellent support, but the school was really tough on students. It was a high-pressure environment for everyone. I was always being watched and never had downtime. In my opinion, one can only live with this kind of pressure for a limited time. Teachers are not afraid to work hard, but we need space to breathe!

However, that experience taught me to really take the science of education seriously, to study the evidence and research. The accountability taught me to look at the science, to explore the effects of poverty, family structure, community, partnerships—to look at the whole child. I built on the foundation of my first teaching job, and because of my practices, I received various awards, including a Certificate of Special Congressional Recognition from the U.S. House of Representatives.

After three years in Miami-Dade in a secondary and post-secondary setting, I went back to a school in Broward County. The situation was worse than the one I left back in 2012. Schools are chasing test scores and students are functioning on autopilot. The current content and process to teach children just do not work. These kids are highly intelligent, very aware of what's going on. But they have been trained by the system to believe that going to school is the only option they have to get a job, and that the system knows what they need better than they do.

These children can do so much today with the abilities and skills they have, but the environment in which they are being taught does not nurture them. My colleagues and I observe it every day. At the age of 2, a child can access so much content with tech, can manipulate it better than we can, and can utilize it in so many ways. These kids are superintelligent, minigeniuses by the age of 5 or 6 because of the information they have access to and what they do with it.

Between ages 2 and 6, children are so creative and imaginative. We have a great opportunity to nurture these children to become creative, innovative problem-solvers who can tackle the big issues in the world. We need to nurture children to live up to their destiny. Our education system does not realize that our children are all gifted.

From the "trenches," my plea to education leaders is this: We need a system shake-up. We are just maintaining the status quo, and forward-thinkers are unable to get traction within leadership. We need a shake-up in content, instructional models, and strategies. I just don't see the system using science to connect education to what is going on today.

Whatever children are learning today, they are learning about the past, where all the questions have already been answered. Instead, we ought to be asking questions today to solve today's problems, which will impact our future. If I were the state's superintendent, I would:

- challenge the way education is systematized today;

- change testing. I don't think a child's future should depend on a content assessment. We can assess a child in other ways that nurture their potential;
- pilot various innovations in education that are far from traditional schooling;
- work with universities to test educational theories; and
- partner with local companies. These stakeholders must support our schools. After all, our workforce is being formed here.

I hear all the time that we do not have the budget for this or the budget for that. If we want to move this country forward in light years, and set a path to prosperity, we need to invest in our children.

Being a teacher is tough. To be an educator is a calling. You can change lives in many ways, even beyond the classroom as an administrator, virtual coach, or through your own strategies. We need teachers! The greatest people who changed the course of history were educators: Buddha, Jesus, Gandhi, and so many others. There will always be a need for teachers.

This is what I want to say to new teachers: It is cliché, but we don't do it for the money. Unfortunately, it might be many years until we get the respect. You have to come in well-aware that there will be days you want to quit, that you will bump heads with administration and colleagues, and you will see things that are almost inhumane. If you want to see an impact, you have to start with yourself, pulling from deep inside. You are making a difference. Little things you say to your students may make a difference.

Children will remember you for that, not for the content you are teaching them. Some of my former students come to me today and say, "You spoke to us about life and how you understood us." My students thank me, even if it is just a small number of students.

Kids recognize teachers who care. They sometimes have lived more than we have because of their circumstances. They've seen so much in such a short period. They know which teachers are not really teaching or who do not care. They also know who really cares. They will do anything for you, as long as you show them you respect them as a decent person, and treat them as human beings. The reward of being a teacher is to be part of another person's journey, to help them fulfill their destiny and purpose in life. As a teacher, you will not be a millionaire, unless you win the lottery! Education is a calling.

I have so many memories of my students. One, in particular, inspired me to continue in this profession when I was having doubts. I established a club called "The Darfur Dream Team" to fundraise for clothes, supplies, and learning materials for children in Chad, a country experiencing a civil war at that time. We had emotional posters all over the campus. My students were not aware of how children might be traumatized during war. Once they understood, they were ready to fundraise.

This particular student shared with me that she wanted to become a lawyer. I remembered that when I was her age, I already wanted to become a teacher, but never had the opportunity to share this passion with my teachers. I was so happy to help her and guide her toward this goal. Two years later, she earned a scholarship to become a human rights attorney. I made a difference in her life and in many others'.

I really hope principals, teachers, and leaders read this message. We must think of the whole child. Let's stop making self-interested decisions. Let's listen to our students' voices, along with the voices of teachers who care, and we will be immensely blessed as teachers and as a nation with the benefits that a proper education brings to students.

The plight of a teacher is the plight of a hero. Teachers face challenges unlike those in any other career as they strive to serve children. What if we could help teachers right away without having to change the school system?

CHAPTER 4

SHOULD WE CLOSE ALL SCHOOLS?

"The difference between school and life? In school, you are taught a lesson and then given a test. In life, you are given a test that teaches you a lesson."

~Tom Bodett

What do you think? Should we close all schools? I wonder if you will feel differently by the time you finish reading this chapter.

Back in the early 1950s, the New York Department of Education asked Albert Einstein what schools should emphasize. Einstein was living in Princeton, New Jersey, at that time, serving as a professor at Princeton University. He already had decades of media exposure worldwide and had become popularly known as a genius. His opinion mattered because he was a man who demonstrated his capacity to explore the unknown. Einstein had an answer and some thoughtful advice:

> *"[Schools should emphasize] teaching history. There should be extensive discussion of personalities who benefited mankind through independence of character and judgment. . . . Critical comment by students should be taken in a friendly spirit. Accumulation of material should not stifle students' independence."*[23]

Einstein summarized the education he would love to have received in school. Reading in between the lines, one can understand that he wanted schools to model successful people, to identify the habits they had, and to help children learn those habits. He wanted schools to foster inquiry, and to focus on imagination over pure content. Indeed, every invention, product, design, piece of art or music, outstanding leader, athlete, book, or movie started in the mind of *one* person. Someone dreamt about something and took action to give life to it. It is that simple. It means the genius is already within the person, just waiting to flourish.

Schools are the ideal place to get children started, to allow them to make mistakes, to help them get back on their feet, and to guide them toward realizing their potential. Perhaps, back in the 1950s, Einstein imagined the future as it is today, as well-connected as the atoms he studied for so long. He predicted that we would need to anchor ourselves in creativity and imagination to design the world that we live in.

In 2010, 60 years after Einstein's recommendations to the New York Department of Education, creativity expert Sir Ken Robinson presented one of the world's most watched and impactful YouTube videos about education, *Changing Education Paradigms*. He shared how every country in the world was undertaking education reform and where they were focusing. Robinson discussed the misalignment between what our children need and the school system countries were reshaping to fulfill the 21st-century's requirements. His message created the awareness we needed to move forward with school reforms. Yet, years later, we have not made significant strides. We do have "pockets of innovation" in isolated schools, but we have seen little to no capacity to scale these innovations.

~ HOW PUBLIC SCHOOLS' HISTORY HOLDS US BACK ~

Mandatory public schooling started in Europe in 1524, as proposed by Martin Luther, who believed it would be an effective way to indoctrinate children into his new Lutheran church. He convinced politicians that public schooling would strengthen state power, and convinced families it would provide equal opportunities for all children to become educated and, therefore, have a greater chance to succeed socially and economically.

The "factory school" model as we know it was first conceived in 1717 by Prussia's King Frederick William I, who paved the way for countries around the world to adopt the same model. Public school systems organized to prepare students as a group, all following the same format and curriculum, at the same time. School hasn't changed much from that 18th-century format, although there is plenty of research and practice that says it needs to change.

Families were convinced schooling was the greatest opportunity their children had for a better life, and this belief has endured throughout the centuries. That's why, since we were young, so many of us were taught to study hard, work hard, be righteous, have a family, buy a house, have a nice vacation here and there, and eventually retire to finally check the box of being prosperous and happy. This is the definition of success that someone else designed, and it had to begin with studying hard in school. Of course, no one outright told us that we could only be entirely successful at the end of life! We were taught to go from birth to death without causing too much trouble to anyone.

With school as our defined access point for this success, we went off at the age of 5 to start working on our life journey in kindergarten. There, teachers told us exactly what to do to be successful throughout our school years: the animals to paint, the subjects to learn, the books to read, the tests to take, the colleges to attend, the jobs to choose, and so on. We were destined to spend most of our time in "automatic mode," on a totally unconscious journey, believing we were doing the right thing. The certainty of this journey can be very comfortable, which conditions us to avoid uncertainty; but the world is unpredictable and uncertain—the opposite of what we were educated for.

Passion was ignored at school, as it is so subjective. After all, there are only a handful of people who reached professional success following their passion. It is too risky for learners to invest in it. We learned to dismiss our deepest desires and to fulfill someone else's definition of success without even noticing it. Isn't it ironic that so many commencement speeches include advice like: "Follow your passion! Listen to your heart!" When did we learn to follow our passion? Do learners even have a passion? How can we ask learners to listen to their hearts when they can barely hear the beats?

The tiniest decisions we make and the actions we take in schools have a significant impact on students' lives. Imagine telling learners precisely what to do during each moment of the day for 12 years. This builds conformism instead of uniqueness. It kills initiative, creativity, and action and can hold back their brains for the rest of their lives. Just following orders becomes natural for students, as they practice it for so long. Students may become afraid of having the initiative to do anything outside of the status quo or to pursue their dreams, because they will be judged for it. They hesitate to do anything that doesn't align with the instructions they receive, because doing so might lead to them being labeled as a failure. Too often, a student who is nonconformist in this way may be medicated with drugs such as Ritalin, so they can go through school like a "normal child."

This is what students are practicing at schools today, and this is what failing organizations still repeat and cultivate in adulthood. A pyramidal chain of command, where bosses set the orders because they know better, is a reflection of the industrial school system in which teachers are the source of knowledge. Employees follow orders by the book, doing only what is necessary to "survive," focusing on fixing errors and mistakes rather than seeking excellence. After all, that is what they have learned through exams, where teachers point out mistakes with that red pen.

This isn't the kind of education students need for today's world. I'll share an example from my own life: My first real job was with a start-up, at the age of 18, while attending college. We were four people and, although I was hired to develop software, we had to do pretty much everything, from answering the phone to serving coffee to clients, creating presentations, and writing proposals. That is life at a start-up. One day, my manager asked me to send a proposal to a customer via fax. Yes, it was a long time ago, and no, we did not have email then. I asked my manager for the fax number. She replied, "I don't know. You find out!" That mundane interaction changed my life. I realized I had always been told what to do and been provided with the tools to do it, but in the real world things work differently. In the real world, we each must find the resources we need and we must make things happen. It took me a while, but I found the customer's fax number.

This experience made me aware that I needed to take action to make things happen. I became uneasy with the ordinary, with merely following orders. I wanted to become a more significant contributor to the world by using simple actions to make things extraordinary. From then on, I began taking the initiative to act based on my observations of what was needed. It eventually paid off, as I became a business partner in the company, and later, after selling my shares in the start-up, had a successful career in corporate America.

~ THE LONG-TERM CONSEQUENCES OF DISCONNECTING LEARNING FROM PASSION ~

In that same year of my first real job, a friend invited me to a concert. I was so tired that weekend, but I went anyway. It turned out to be an amazing experience! Brazilian singer Ludmila Ferber and her band engaged us for hours that felt like minutes. Ferber's voice sounded like the waves of the ocean on a calm, full-moon night. She handled the tonal changes so easily. Her lyrics, which she wrote herself, joined the melody and shot straight from the brain to the heart.

At the end of the concert, my friend managed to take us backstage and I had a chance to talk to Ferber. "I want to sing like you. How can I sing like you?" I asked her. I had always loved music and the concert inspired me. She asked me back: "What do you want for your life? What is your passion?" I stared at her with my mouth open. "What? I don't know!" I answered, shrugging my shoulders. "I am attending college to become an engineer. Is that okay?" She looked at me, deep in my eyes, and said, "When you figure out what your passion is, come talk to me again." Ferber turned away and I wished in that moment I could have spelled out my passion.

I didn't have a passion at that time. I was told what to do my entire life. I thought the choice to become an engineer translated into "passion," but truly, I had no clue. I have seen my story repeated in so many students' lives, and my work is about changing that.

Little by little, schools disconnect children from their passion, as shown in the creative genius-related study by Dr. George Land described in chapter 2. Being told to learn something unrelated to their interests or passion causes learners boredom, exam stress, and diminished excitement about learning. As students grow up with this model, many of them will experience falling levels of the neurotransmitters serotonin and dopamine in their brains. The body gets used to this blend of chemicals.[24] Serotonin is responsible for satisfaction, and dopamine is responsible for excitement. Lower levels of these neurotransmitters result in apathy, lack of motivation, lack of interest, anxiety for an uncertain future, and depression.

By no means am I saying that schools are the only cause of students' depression and anxiety. Nevertheless, we must recognize that students spend a significant part of their young years at school, and what happens in this environment plays a vital role in their development. School directly influences the brain, based on what children learn, listen to, engage with, and experience.

Regardless of the cause, our schools are serving a generation with high levels of anxiety and depression. During the past 25 years, depression and anxiety among teens have increased by 70%.[25] The *Journal of Social & Personal Relationships* reported these teens are the "loneliest generation"—only 28% spend time with friends daily and 38% often feel lonely. In a late 2018 Pew Research Center poll, 70% of teens ages 13 to 17 said that depression and anxiety were a significant issue among their peers.

Take a moment to examine this situation for yourself. Did you experience stress and anxiety while you were in school? What about your peers—what was their emotional condition during exams, finals, and papers? There is a good chance that many in your group, including you, experienced these undesired emotions. Now imagine the impact of these experiences as young people mature into the workforce without the tools and skills to handle their own emotional states. The impact globally is so large that the World Economic Forum has reported that around 4% of the global population is diagnosed with anxiety disorders. It also estimates that 62% of people do not receive any treatment for their disorder, and that by 2030, mental health issues will cost the global economy $16 trillion.[26]

The bad news is that the lack or surplus of one or more neurotransmitters in the brain can become an addiction for the body, creating an eternal loop of imbalance. Prescription and recreational drugs or alcohol stimulate the production of neurotransmitters such as epinephrine, dopamine, and serotonin, giving the user the sensation of well-being. However, once the drugs' effects disappear, the imbalance returns, thus addicting the user to the drug in order to produce the related neurotransmitters.

Anxiety and depression, or a continuous dose of norepinephrine from any source, diminish the motivation to do things such as work, exercise, or relate to others. They increase blood pressure by putting the body in a near-constant "fight or flight" state, and they increase the appetite for "comfort food," which can lead to heart diseases. When this begins in childhood or the teen years, it generally persists through adulthood.[27]

For too many students, school numbs their brains, causing dissatisfaction, boredom, stress, and anxiety whose source they cannot identify. The result? Indifference, which they carry with them into the work world and turn into deliberate disengagement. This represents $300 billion in annual lost productivity, according to a 2013 Gallup report. More than 87% of Americans are actively disengaged at work. Are they following their passion and realizing their dreams? The numbers say otherwise.

It is a rough reality. The more we are disconnected from what we love and the pleasure of engaging with it, the bigger the negative impact on the rest of our years. Land, Sagan, Robinson, and so many others have warned us that this is happening in our schools. Is the solution to close all schools, then? In my humble opinion, absolutely not. Nevertheless, spending another day educating children as we do today, in a system where rigor prevails over relevance, is a waste of potential and of talented minds. What to do?

I am not qualified to dictate how schools should function or what they should look like. But I present this to you from my experience working in education, from my expertise in technology, from my understanding of what is coming with artificial intelligence, and from a commitment to building something valuable together.

First and foremost, we must stop talking about closing schools, blaming teachers or students, or even blaming the system. The more time we spend complaining, the less time we are taking action. Second, we must understand that it is incredibly challenging to change a system that is two centuries old. Therefore, let us replace "change" with "growth" in our vocabulary. Yes, the current system was conceived for the industrial era. But when the knowledge era came along, it did not replace the industrial era, but, rather, grew from it. So it should be with the education system, which can grow from the conveyer-belt school format to the fostering-potential school format. Third, we must take action and make it happen, envisioning the system's scalability.

~ HOW WE CAN MAKE SCHOOL BETTER RIGHT NOW ~

We can address the disconnection of learning from passion, and the subsequent disengagement at work, with the generations being schooled now. Regardless of where we are today with any given school system, the brain's neuroplasticity allows human beings to change their behavior, mood, and view of life. When neurotransmitters fire, it is an action potential. The way we act and react to it will create a balance or imbalance of neurotransmitters. Certain kinds of psychological therapy, for instance, give us the cognitive awareness to control our thoughts and actions.

Simply practicing to change a reaction toward a particular reward when a bad habit is cued will eventually replace the bad habit with a good one.

The good results of therapy directly influence the economy: a $4 return in work productivity for every $1 invested in treating mental disorders.[28] In the same vein, positive experiences can help change the balance of neurotransmitters in the mind, just as negative ones can. This is well demonstrated through the science of neuroplasticity, also known as brain plasticity. It has shown that our activities, experiences—positive or negative—and myriad other factors can trigger our brains to grow new neural connections, strengthen existing ones, and speed up transmissions between neurons. These changes can happen at any age.[29]

For younger generations, a positive school experience can contribute to a healthy balance of neurotransmitters. Children must unlearn the idea that they are born with certain qualities that define who they will be in life. They must instead learn they can develop the capacity to be whoever they want to be. Research by psychologist and Stanford professor Dr. Carol Dweck shows that these kinds of teachings lead children to develop two very different mindsets:[30]

- **Fixed mindset:** When they are taught or treated as if they're born with certain unchangeable qualities, "students believe their basic abilities, their intelligence, their talents, are just fixed traits," Dweck explains; and

- **Growth mindset:** When children are taught that they can get smarter, that their brains can grow and change, "they believe everyone can get smarter if they work at it," Dweck says.

A fixed mindset urges perfection and relates rewards to doing precisely what teachers say. A perfectionist is their own worst critic, continuously trying to be worthy, only accepting others based on limited characteristics. Dweck's research shows this leads students to focus on looking smart all the time, on never looking dumb or trying something that might not work.

When guided toward a growth mindset, on the other hand, students "understand that their talents and abilities can be developed through effort, good teaching, and persistence. They don't necessarily think everyone's the same or anyone can be Einstein, but they believe everyone can get smarter if they work at it," Dweck explains. This causes them to put in the passionate, engaged time and effort that leads to higher achievement.

If children learn that failing is part of the process of growing as a human being, they are likely to share more about what happens to them and what motivates them, thus giving adults better clues to guide their development. One important, free, fast, and effective way that educators can make the school experience better is to actively guide children toward a growth mindset, where each child starts from their current point of development.

Following below are five points that I invite you to consider about improving the school experience from a pedagogical perspective. Certainly, there are other areas to consider, such as infrastructure, teachers' compensation, resources, and so on. Nevertheless, during the last 15 years I have seen education communities find a way to greatly improve students' lives when starting from these points. These are often underserved schools, where teachers create their own books because the system does not provide them with textbooks. They are schools with no technology, where students find a way to research the latest news. They are overcrowded schools where teachers and students work together to help each other and get everyone to learn. If these schools were able to be successful, imagine schools with all the available resources! There is no excuse for not trying.

~ FIVE KEY FOUNDATIONS FOR IMPROVING PEDAGOGY ~

1. **The system already exists.**

We must start from where we are, from our current practices, from what we know. There are many processes and procedures already in place. My objective is for you to adopt practices aligned to existing policies and then transform policies as you see results and master these practices. For example, advocating to eliminate standardized tests all at once is a waste of time. Instead, strive to demonstrate through action that students will gain more from time and attention given to self-evaluation. Then, policies will eventually evolve to reflect this.

2. **School must help each child find and pursue their purpose in life.**

To increase excitement about learning, children must continuously learn things associated with their passions, at home and at school. This naturally produces dopamine in their brains, creating a cycle of positive reinforcement for more learning. For example, do you know why many children dislike reading? Because it involves reading books they do not enjoy. Reading a book unrelated to your passion is as dull as reading a manual; you read it once, maybe, to learn how to operate something, and then dismiss it with the hope you'll never touch it again. Instead, encourage children to read books related to their individual interests. The conscious and subconscious must work together in learning. The language of the subconscious is emotions and forms, which is why effective learning involves what we love.

3. **Social exposure helps children learn.**

Have you noticed how young children accelerate their speaking when they start pre-K? This social exposure allows them to share knowledge and learn behaviors from each other. It is the social cognitive theory of Stanford University professor of psychology Dr. Albert Bandura, which we will discuss in the upcoming chapters. Children will evolve faster when they are in a learning community of different ages, skills, and interests.[31]

4. **Students must have control of their own learning process.**

Pedagogy researchers have been exploring new learning methodologies for decades. Some are more prominent than others, but all of them include the influence of the "coach" in the learning process: Project-based learning allows students to discover their passions through individual and group experiences. Personalized learning aligns students' learning experience to their passions. Competency-based learning fosters necessary skill development. Autonomous learning enables students to learn the practices they will use for life.

When we learn to take control of the learning process, we can adjust and control any situation. A growth mindset focuses on the process, while a fixed mindset focuses on the outcome. Deliberate practice of the learning process will develop cognitive, socioemotional, and personal skills. Read more about this in chapter 9.

5. **Students need a continuous practice of metacognition—thinking about how one thinks.**

Teaching children the skill of metacognition leads to the self-evaluation of their progress at each step of the learning process. It creates self-awareness of their actions, of the effort on a task, of the quality of their work, and of the alignment of their work with their passions. When they use metacognition as part of the learning process, students understand what they are capable of and how much they can push themselves. They will refine their sensitivity in observing where to improve. Metacognition develops resilience, self-esteem, divergent thinking, and more.[31] Bandura calls this process a guided mastery, in which teachers support students in altering beliefs about what they can accomplish—one small, manageable step at a time.

We discussed earlier in this chapter that every invention, product, design, piece of art or music, outstanding leader, athlete, book, or movie started in the mind of *one* person. You can be this person, by starting to imagine the school where children develop creative confidence, blossom as healthy human beings, are motivated to realize their dreams, and are confident they have the skills to do so. Why not?

The future reserves the role of creation for us, so let us embrace it. Let us join forces and equip learners to flourish their innate genius throughout their lives. You and I can arm learners with the tools to make them successful. And their success is our success as individuals and as a nation.

CHAPTER 5

UNDERSTANDING INTELLIGENCE

"You've got to win in your mind
before you win in your life."

~JOHN ADDISON

"I don't get it. When we first got married, you could punch out a breakfast like mother used to make. Now you are all thumbs!" says George Jetson to his wife, Jane Jetson, in an episode[32] of the futuristic family cartoon *The Jetsons*. If you are old enough, you will remember watching it on TV. George wishes his wife would cook him breakfast, rather than use their new breakfast machine. Frustrated, George leaves the room on a rolling carpet, while Jane starts her housework by pushing buttons for robots to do her laundry, ironing, and cleaning, all while she sits in the comfort of her floating chair. In this imagined future, machines do everything for us, leaving considerable spare time for other things. In Jane's case, that means plenty of time to enjoy her obsessions: fashion and new gadgetry. Are we in the future yet?

We use technology in most areas of our lives. Think of your travel experience, for instance. You have full access to everything through your mobile phone: your boarding pass, the airplane's movies, a text message with the location of your rental car, the digital key for your hotel room, food from a restaurant nearby. While you use them, these apps are learning about your preferences, recording data that can be analyzed at any time so to offer you similar or new items or services you are likely to consume.

The more you interact with apps, the more they learn from you. With enough data, apps can predict the products and services that will better serve you, wherever you are. This interaction-based data analysis is called artificial intelligence (AI). Its developers hope it will replace the salesperson at the shoe store, the manager at the bookstore, and maybe even the sommelier at a fancy restaurant. You, in turn, are no longer annoyed by advertising because you actually like what you are being offered.

AI is a part of your daily life. From the local supermarket club card to ads in your web browser, you are sharing personal preferences in exchange for value, such as discounts or free services. It is the new normal, and you like it! Consider YouTube: You watch a video and, like magic, the right column is filled with dozens more videos on the same topic. How about Netflix? Have you ever noticed the same movie presented to you with different scenes? It is exploring your preferences, learning which image catches your attention and makes you click. Coincidence? Nope, it's AI.

In education, some may think the applicability of AI is to replace classroom teachers. Indeed, there are many companies testing this very concept. Others are using AI in their apps to personalize content according to students' weaknesses or to build a "learning playlist" called adaptive learning. To date, however, there is little to no evidence that AI is effective in education. With adaptive learning, which makes the most use of AI at this time, students may remember something for a test, but there is no guarantee they actually learned content that will be useful for them, or that they learned a new skill.

In previous chapters, I discussed the genius within your students and how you can be the catalyst for them realizing their potential. I also discussed the importance of schools in this process. Now, with the growing role of technology in our lives, how can we make use of AI to truly benefit learners? First, we need to understand how biological intelligence (BI) and artificial intelligence work, and then how they interact.

~ BIOLOGICAL INTELLIGENCE ~

Our brains are the most complex organs to understand. There is so much yet to be discovered! Now, bear with me as we dive into some brain biology that will help you understand some of the science behind a new framework of learning.

For the purpose of this book, we'll simplify the brain into four main parts:

- **Prefrontal cortex**: responsible for knowledge and subjective consciousness;
- **Midbrain**: in charge of emotions, habits, and the subconscious mind;
- **Cerebellum**: where our memories and objective consciousness reside; and
- **Brainstem**: responsible for communication between the brain and the body.

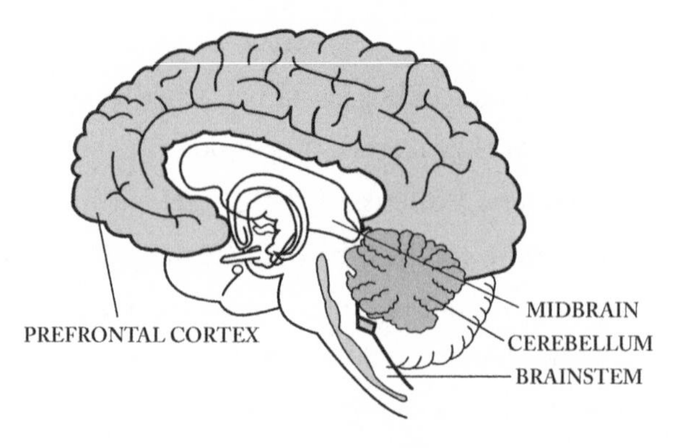

Figure 5.1: The brain's four main parts

The brain has 100 billion neurons working in synchrony to give life to your reality. It's like the melody of the most beautiful song you have ever heard. Each neuron has dendrites (head extremity), an axon (body), and axon terminals (lower extremity.) At the cellular level, when we learn something new that interests us, neurons get "excited" and connect their axon terminals to dendrites of other neurons via a synaptic connection, which is "glued" by neurotransmitters such as dopamine, serotonin, and norepinephrine. The neurotransmitters are responsible for "exciting" the neuron. The stronger the neuron's excitement, the "harder" the connection to other neurons.

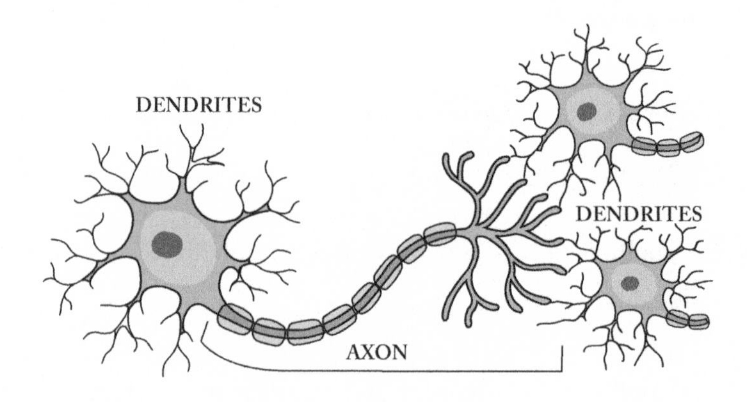

Figure 5.2: A neuron connection

More than 60 types of neurotransmitters—or glues—have been identified to date, divided into excitatory, inhibitory, or both. Excitatory neurotransmitters increase the activity of the neuron after the synaptic connection; inhibitory neurotransmitters decrease activity of the neuron after the connection. Although neurotransmitters are classified within six types, we will only focus on three types that associated with learning: monoamines, peptides, and amino acids.

Monoamines include four critical neurotransmitters:

1. **Epinephrine, or adrenaline** (excitatory and inhibitory), is both a neurotransmitter and a hormone responsible for excitement or stress. The body can only handle a few hours of excitement or stress; too much epinephrine can lead to anxiety and too little can lead to depression.

2. **Norepinephrine** (excitatory and inhibitory) is the neurotransmitter associated with the "fight or flight response," an alertness reaction to danger or stress. A lack or surplus of norepinephrine has the same effects as epinephrine.

3. **Dopamine** (inhibitory) coordinates body movements and pleasurable sensations such as rewards, motivation, and attention.

4. **Serotonin** (excitatory) regulates and modulates emotional states, sleep, anxiety, sexuality, and appetite. A lack of serotonin can make one anxious, and too much of it can be seen in people with autism. Antidepressant drugs bring back the levels of serotonin in the brain, improving mood and reducing the feeling of anxiety.

Peptides include two neurotransmitters:

1. **Oxytocin** is both a hormone and a neurotransmitter, associated with social recognition, bonding, and sexual attraction. It is often referred to as the "hormone of love."

2. **Endorphins** promote the feeling of euphoria and positive emotions, and inhibit pain signals. They respond to pain, stress, fear, pleasure, exercise, meditation, and other stimuli, and are both excitatory and inhibitory. A lack of endorphins can create or magnify pain, depression, anxiety, moodiness, trouble sleeping, and other issues. A surplus can create an artificial "high" state. Endorphins play a part in everything from addictions to diabetes to brain aging.

Finally, the **amino acids** include two neurotransmitters:

1. **Gamma-aminobutyric acid (GABA)** (inhibitory) regulates vision, motor control, and anxiety. It helps to offset excitatory messages and regulates daily sleep-wake cycles. Prescription drugs for anxiety increase the efficiency of GABA, which brings feelings of relaxation and calm.

2. **Glutamate** (excitatory) plays a vital role in cognitive functions such as memory and learning. There is more glutamate in the nervous system than any other neurotransmitter, meaning we are continuously learning!

Effective learning of new knowledge starts in our right frontal lobe, in the prefrontal cortex. Our understanding of this new knowledge connects neurons, by either growing an existing neural network or forming a new one. We then must practice the new knowledge to strengthen synaptic connections. The more excited we are about the new knowledge, the stronger the neural connections. The more we practice the new skill, the higher the chance it will become a habit. This new "skill" is then stored in the midbrain or cerebellum for later use.[33]

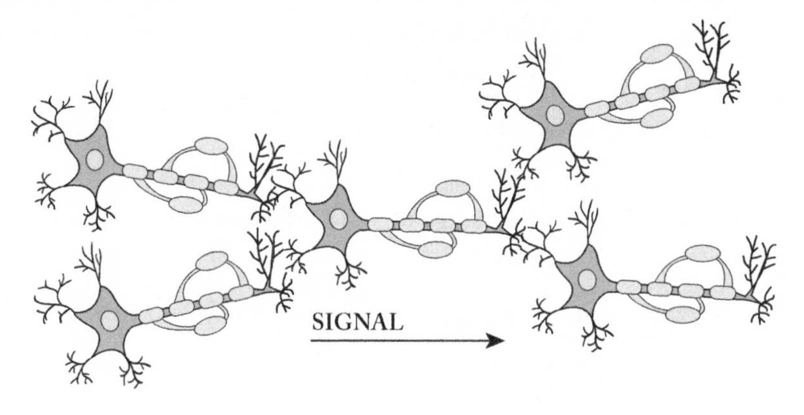

Figure 5.3: A neural network

Through extensive research, Dr. Donald Hebb, often considered the "father of neuroscience," discovered we learn faster when we associate new knowledge with previous knowledge. This means connecting neurons to existing neural networks in our brains. Thus, Hebb wrote, "cells that fire together, wire together."[34] For example, if you want to learn how to ski, your instructor might teach you to align your skis like a slice of pizza to stop, and like french fries to move. You will understand the concept of skiing by associating it with food geometry, and will be able to stop and go with pizza and french fries! Practice will strengthen your skiing neural network and eventually skiing will become natural to you, a skill stored in your cerebellum that you can use whenever you want by "turning on" this specific sequence of neural networks.

We can use this knowledge of the brain's learning system to benefit learners by creating units of study with four learning stages. These stages take advantage of how neurons connect to each other. Continuous practice of this learning process throughout the school years enables students to learn anything they want during their lives.

The four learning stages:

1. **Explore** previous knowledge that connects to the new knowledge, and understand the purpose and value of what is learned. "Cells that fire together, wire together";

2. **Research** new knowledge to fully understand its concepts;

3. **Practice** new knowledge to strengthen synaptic connections, by using exercises, an essay, teamwork, a project, games, or other types of activities; and

4. **Relate** the new knowledge to one's own life to discover its practical applicability, answering the question: "How can I use what I learned?" It will eventually become a skill or habit.

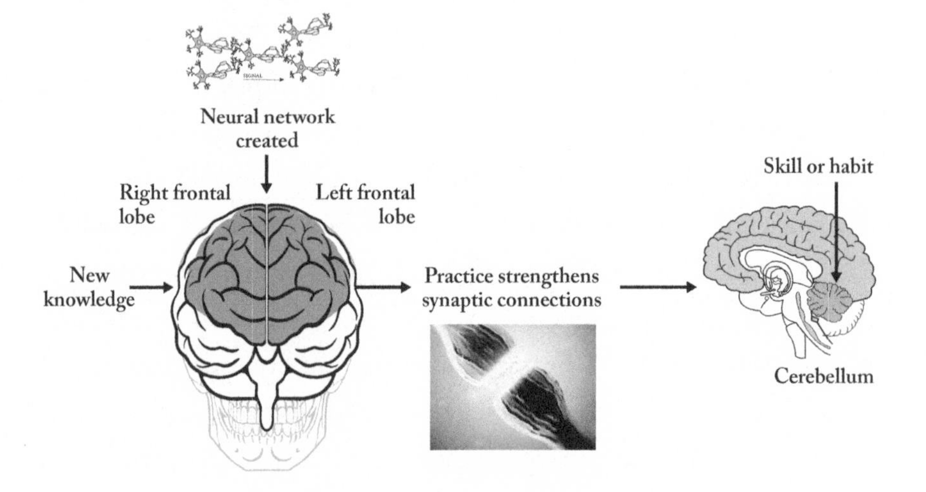

Figure 5.4: How learning occurs

You can access sample units of study that use these four learning stages on our website, BecomingEinsteinsTeacher.com. We will deep dive into this concept in chapters 9 and 10.

~ ARTIFICIAL INTELLIGENCE ~

George Boole (1815–1864) had only formal primary education. He was forced to drop out of school when his father's business started to decline. His father was a science lover and "homeschooled" little Boole with everything he knew. What he learned the most from his father, though, was to be curious, to ask questions, and to seek answers. His father's friends helped the boy by lending him books, and one of these friends even taught him Latin. He later taught himself four more languages and, by the age of 12, published the translation of a Greek poem in the local newspaper. Many called him an impostor, as they could not believe a 12-year-old British boy spoke Greek.

By the age of 16, Boole was the sole provider for his parents and three younger siblings, working as a junior teacher at a local school in Lincoln, England. Math continued to intrigue him; the more he learned, the more he was curious. While working at a boarding school, he published his first paper "*On the origin, progress, and tendencies of Polytheism, especially amongst the ancient Egyptians and Persians, and in modern India*" on November 30, 1841. It was the start of his stellar career. His later work won him the first-ever mathematics prize from the Royal Society. He became a Royal Society fellow in 1857 and received honorary degrees from the University of Dublin and the University of Oxford.

Boole's first book, *The Laws of Thought* (1854), established the mathematical theories of logic and probabilities. He proposed that the way we think is by logic. He had an interest in how people live, work, and think, and translated it into simple mathematical rules and concepts.

You may recall from your math classes Boolean algebra, or Boolean logic, in which the value of variables is either true (1) or false (0). Little did he know how his theories would be used for centuries to follow!

George Boole laid the foundation for information technology. Without his work, there would be no computers or cell phones, as we know them today. Dr. Claude Shannon (1916–2001), an American mathematician and electrical engineer, and Dr. Victor Shestakov (1907–1987), a Russian logician and theoretician of electrical engineering, proposed in 1938 and 1941, respectively, the design of the digital circuit using Boole's logic. This was the theoretical grounding for the information age. There is not one piece of technology or programming language that does not use Boolean logic. A simple chip made of silicon and wires can do many tasks that previously required human thought. Although Boole died of pneumonia at the age of 49, he lived long enough to become the grandfather of artificial intelligence.

Scientists from IBM, Carnegie Mellon University, and the Massachusetts Institute of Technology (MIT) created the term "artificial intelligence" in 1956. It is the "ability" computers have to mimic humans' cognitive functions, especially problem solving. AI does not think. It just uses algorithms to analyze data and suggest logic pathways. Algorithms are procedures with a finite number of steps, and they frequently repeat a particular operation using data, like following a cake recipe. The data is the ingredients and the algorithm is the recipe. Therefore, AI helps us with repetitive tasks, improving our efficiency because of the many steps saved along the way. The more data inputs the AI possesses, the more precise the algorithm will be.

In 2015, Nigel Richards won the French World Scrabble Championship.[35] Nigel is from New Zealand, does not speak French, and has low to no ability to read a book in French. He memorized the French dictionary with the sole objective of playing Scrabble. Nigel is a living human version of AI! Like playing Scrabble, any job that can be performed as an algorithm or a sequence of steps, can be replaced by AI.

There are four basic concepts to understand about AI:

1. **Big Data**: Think of a "big brother" observing your preferences and taking notes on everything you chose. Data is organized in datasets to be used later.

2. **Machine Learning**: Data is collected to build upon your preferences or to suggest related things. For example, when you Google search "artificial intelligence," the results will include articles related to technology, research, courses, news, and AI's definition. All of these topics relate to AI.

3. **Neural Networks**: Algorithms use a significant amount of data from various interactions you have with different apps. Using the previous example, Google will show you what other people input when they search for "artificial intelligence." AI neural networks are this combination of interests, linked by a more substantial amount of data. And yes, the term "neural networks" derives from our brains' neural networks. Another example of a neural network at work is the "Customers Who Bought This Item Also Bought" section on Amazon.com. Have you ever had the curiosity to click on one of those suggestions? AI helped you to get there!

4. **Deep Neural Networks or Deep Learning**: This uses many-layered neural networks to build algorithms that perform tasks on their own, based on vast sets of data. To experience deep neural networks, go to your photos on Facebook, and it will

tell you to tag yourself in photos or ask you to tag a friend by their name, regardless of whether the photo is recent or 20 years old. Face recognition or the diagnosis of pancreatic cancer are examples of deep learning.

~ WHY AI MEANS WE NEED LEARNING HABITS MORE THAN EVER ~

Dr. Larry R. Squire, a professor of psychiatry, neurosciences, and psychology at the University of California, San Diego, has led significant research about memory and habits. Squire and his team studied patient Eugene Pauly for 14 years after Eugene lost part of his brain's functions to viral encephalitis. Eugene could not remember facts and events that has happened recently or just a couple of minutes previously, but had a vivid memory of his life before the age of 25. He could not explain how to get from the bedroom to the kitchen in his house, although he could walk to the kitchen and grab something to eat whenever he was hungry. He did not know his address, or how to describe getting to his house. However, after his wife accompanied him for a while on a routine morning walk in the neighborhood, he could walk by himself and come back home, never getting lost.

Squire's team concluded that, even though part of the brain may be inoperative, it can still develop habits. He based his conclusions on the work of MIT researchers who were exploring how habits were formed. Those researchers implanted tiny sensors in rats' brains to observe minor changes there. During the experiment, researchers would place a piece of chocolate at one end of a maze. A loud noise would sound, followed by the opening of a door to the maze. With the door opened, the rats would wander for a while doing what rats do: sniffing around to find the next exciting thing. Eventually, the rats would find the chocolate. Researchers observed high activity in the rats' prefrontal cortexes and midbrains while they were in the process of "discovery." Once they learned within a week where the chocolate was, the rats would navigate through the maze directly to the reward as soon as the noise sounded and the door opened, with no wrong turns. Their brains showed a decrease in mental activity; the rats knew precisely how to find the chocolate.

This is the recipe for forming a habit. First, a cue triggers our brains about which habit to use. Second, there is an action, either emotional or physical. Finally, there is a reward, which tells our brains whether this habit is worth "recording" to be used in the future. Whenever Eugene felt hungry (cue), he would walk to the kitchen (action), and have something to eat (reward.) In the maze experience, whenever the noise was heard (cue), rats would go into the maze (action) to get their chocolate (reward). Eating is usually a valuable reward (especially chocolate!), so their brains recorded the actions. The continued practice makes these actions habits, which are stored in our subconscious mind and recalled whenever we need them.

Habits are great to have. Otherwise, our brains would go crazy, trying to figure out actions over and over again. Imagine if you had to learn to ride a bike all over again every day! Our brains would have to be huge to carry all the necessary neurons to make that happen. Our subconscious mind registers certain habits forever, such as riding a bike. That is why you probably will never forget how to ride a bike, even if you spend years without practicing it.

The bad news is that our brains do not distinguish good habits from bad habits; they are all the same. Habits are there, just waiting for their cue. The good news is that humans can learn and decide to act upon a cue with conscious awareness. Thus, our brains have the capacity to identify and separate good habits from bad through self-awareness; we can then work to stick to the good ones. This is called cognitive control, "the ability to flexibly adapt behavior to rapidly changing circumstances and to make decisions that best serve long-term interests over more immediate rewards."[36] In other words, it is the deliberate activation and use of the prefrontal cortex. To change bad habits, we must identify the cue, modify the action, ensure the reward for the new habit is enough incentive to create the neural connection, and ensure the reward continues to be experienced.[37]

Like BI, AI also stimulates neurotransmitters, responsible for strengthening our brain's neural network connections. Just notice how Google, Facebook, LinkedIn, Pinterest, Amazon, or Twitter personalize your experience, which stimulates the release of dopamine. This captures your attention, which leads to the release of more dopamine, as well as epinephrine. This release of dopamine generates a sense of satisfaction or pleasure.

This combination of neurotransmitters makes you feel good. The constant novelty of the click increases dopamine levels, and the brain likes it! Consequently, the brain will focus on recreating this valuable experience, seeking out the largest dopamine reward. You become "addicted" to this combination of neurotransmitters and its effect on you, making you "crave" this sensation. The continuous doses of these chemicals generate behaviors that become habits wired in our brains.

If these apps have kidnapped your attention, you have been "hacked" and are now dependent and susceptible to manipulation, with little cognitive control over it. The constant novelty of a click or the sound of a notification on your mobile device increases dopamine levels, thus, making your social media activity a habit and stealing control of your time. You believe more in what you read on these apps than what you see on the TV news. You will most likely buy things offered through these apps. You will be distracted in the middle of an important meeting because your phone vibrated with a new notification. Narcissism may then be born, with you measuring your value by the number of likes you have on Facebook or how many times your phone vibrates with a new notification throughout the day.

Who needs chemical or nuclear bombs when enemies can play with our brain chemicals? We are vulnerable more than ever to AI. It seems like a horror story in which AI can take over the world. This is certainly a possibility, unless we are aware of this effect and understand how to counter it. The only way to be a nonhackable being, one who cannot unknowingly be manipulated by AI, is to use cognitive control.

Here's an example of how I use cognitive control: I use technology extensively to communicate with people all over the world. I am constantly receiving emails, chats from my team, and messages through social media. If I allow my brain to function in automatic mode, I will be checking messages every two minutes, without even thinking. I am aware of this dynamic and make a conscious decision to turn off my phone by 8 p.m. This is cognitive control.

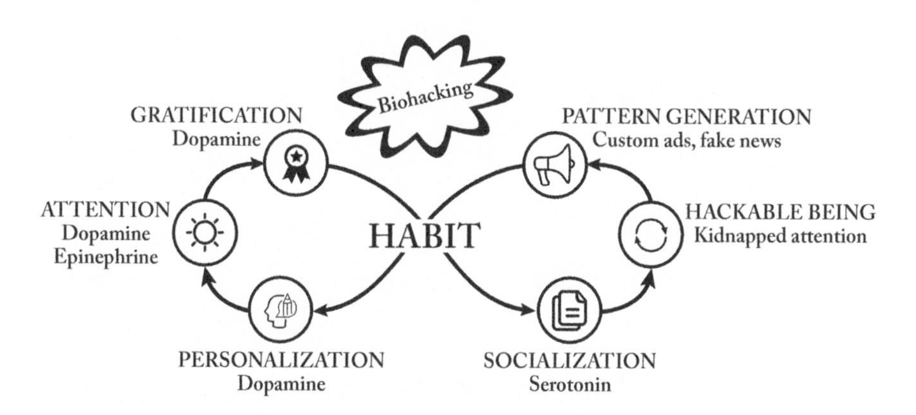

Figure 5.5: When AI creates a habit

Creating a habit is great; however, it has to be a positive habit. To turn students into nonhackable beings, we need to help them develop learning autonomy. Understanding knowledge and applying it improves cognitive control, which enables learners to think, choose, incorporate the right skills to their lives, and, consequently, make wise choices today and in the future.[38]

For example, if we were to develop the habit of "applying past knowledge to new situations," we might make better connections to what we already know. If we were to focus on "thinking flexibly," we could begin to understand the content of what we are learning from multiple perspectives. Those are two of the 16 "Habits of Mind," a set of problem-solving and life-related skills developed by Dr. Arthur L. Costa and Dr. Bena Kallick.[39] Their research showed that these habits, based on intent more than on behavior, develop learners' thinking muscles and agency—both of which are vital in the unknown world AI introduces.

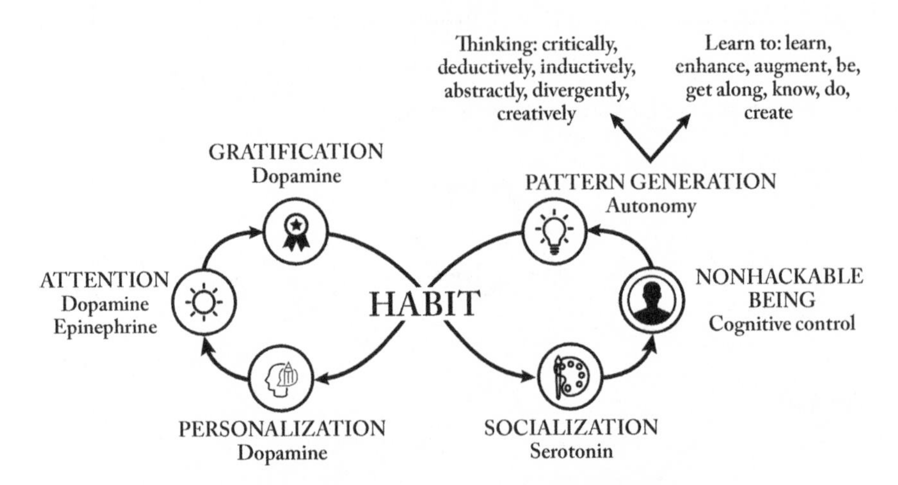

Figure 5.6: When students develop agency

Dopamine, the primary neurotransmitter AI triggers in our brains, is not about pleasure, but, rather, about the anticipation of pleasure. It is about the anticipation of a reward. The less dopamine an activity produces, the less motivation there is to engage in it. The brain focuses on activities that lead to the highest dopamine rewards. That is why your students want to play with their phones when the lecture is boring. When we practice cognitive control, we train the brain to create enough dopamine to reinforce the valuable experience of nonhackable habits. Only when we experience and enjoy the outcome of good habits can we understand how much better they are. We then condition our brain to good habits.

We have worked with thousands of students whose teachers and parents have commented on the way their behavior changed after they started using the Relational Learning Framework in school. Brian, for instance, was diagnosed with ADHD and dyslexia at just 6 years old. He was a very "active" child, and his mother refused to medicate him, although the doctor said it would be the only way to help him attend school. She was also concerned about his future: What would he amount to if he could not read or learn?

Brian was in 2nd grade when we started working with his school. Through professional development, his teachers learned to nurture Brian's cognitive and socioemotional skills with a single process, by using the Relational Learning Framework. We detail this process in chapters 9 and 10. Brian learned to observe himself and figure out his personal talents. He learned to communicate his talents to his teachers and, with their help, improve the skills he possessed. At each step of the process, his brain flooded with rewarding neurotransmitters as he accomplished his goals. This motivated him to learn. Biologically speaking, he received continuous reinforcement of his ability to accomplish things the doctor once denied possible—exactly what he needed to become a self-motivated learner and to put forth the necessary effort.

Two years later, Brian's mother shares with us that she no longer needs to beg Brian to do his schoolwork. He gets home with everything done already! He recently participated in a reading contest, where he performed far better than he had in the past. Moreover, Brian has the initiative to help his mother with household tasks. Brian still has ADHD and dyslexia, but the self-awareness he has developed and practiced allows him to identify when he can learn and when he needs a break. Brian is a happy young teenager with developed cognitive control!

~ APPLYING AI IN EDUCATION ~

While AI can condition bad habits, it also has many positive and practical applications in education:

1. **Making learning a personal experience based on students' preferences.** AI can design learning pathways according to students' individual preferences, thereby increasing their engagement with and interest in learning. AI can create a self-service learning culture. It can highlight what learners are good at and how they can further improve themselves. This personal experience, powered by AI, can replace today's focus on learners' areas for improvement with a focus on their areas of preference, giving each learner the opportunity to grow from where they excel, expanding knowledge from a personal reference point. The more we work on something we love, the more we will be motivated and thus, the higher our chance of succeeding in life.

2. **Organizing content into useful knowledge.** In our connected world, learners interact with numerous apps using their personal identity. AI uses data points of life experience to combine content and present it to learners as a primary reference, something like a personal content curator. This makes learning by association easier, leading to new neuron connections enabled by dopamine, which, in turn, triggers the curiosity to explore more. This

organized content allows learners to make better decisions with immediate application to their real lives. Real-time applicability shifts learning from isolated subjects into a useful resource they can use to improve their choices and better understand solutions for their lives today. Learners must find meaning and value in what they learn.

3. **The new learning experience replaces repeatable habits and fosters creation.** Education is no longer about the regurgitation of content. With the advent of AI, algorithms perform the repetitive task of regurgitation. Education can focus on how learners use knowledge to create and recreate the world around them. Creation has the opportunity to displace procrastination as dopamine excites learners and strengthens neuron connections through practical use of the new knowledge. There is no lack of attention because learning is built around what learners enjoy doing, creating possibilities based upon their choices. If there is an area learners are uninterested in exploring, they will find "experts," who may easily be their peers, not necessarily adults.

4. **It allows education to move from system-centric metrics to student-centric metrics.** Seat time, dropout rates, grades and GPA, do not matter in the AI world! After all, aren't these the metrics of a factory? We must think about augmenting biological intelligence, a process in which learners build knowledge, practice, and new skills aligned with their potential. Imagine a world in which learners choose different learning pathways based on their interests and decision-making. Each learning pathway will give them a "microcredential," which is a seal of expertise

> in a particular area. This recognition of improvement in an area they love will enhance the levels of dopamine and serotonin in the brain, strengthening neural networks even more. Each learner might earn a combination of microcredentials that arm them to make unique contributions to the world, and because of that, they can become irreplaceable. The learning experience is personal, and so are the metrics. At the same time, standardized tests will eventually need to be replaced. While they may have served us well up to now, we need to move toward personalized assessment along with personalized learning. We will explore this concept in more detail in chapter 8.

How might this new, AI-driven, AI-ready, personalized education system play out as students move into the jobs market? It could make hiring the right person easier. Imagine you are the editor-in-chief of the largest newspaper in the country. When hiring a new young reporter to work with you, you may be impressed by a high GPA, but what really matters is the candidate's experience, relevant past work, ability to make deadlines, writing style, third-party endorsements, and so on.

What if you could interview candidates who are passionate about literature and have been writing articles or essays since their early school years? If it takes 10,000 hours to become an expert on anything, these students may have practiced 16,800 hours,[40] coached by their educators during K-12, to gain expertise in what they love. Who would you hire? The young talent with a 4.0 GPA or the young expert who shares with you a portfolio filled with relevant writing? The microcredentials acquired by the latter student may well be critical, deductive, inductive, abstract, divergent, and filled with creative thinking. Their personalized assessments may demonstrate the ability to write pieces on different subjects, set and meet goals, manage their time well, and so on.

We are at an inflection point in history when we can shift the use of AI in education in the right direction. For that, we must make the right choices when deciding which technologies to use in our schools. The proper use of AI develops students' learning autonomy, personalizes their learning process rather than the content, and has the ultimate goal of developing competencies and habits of mind, which will be part of students' lives forever. We must ignore any technology offering more of the same, such as regurgitation of content, old metrics, or learning without student agency.

Until now, learners had access to resources available in schools and technology with vertical content. AI opens their horizons of knowledge, entices their minds to ask more questions, and sparks a desire to explore what they have not thought about. We are continuously creating the world around us through the interpretation of our thoughts. Perhaps AI will enable us to reach the next level of intelligence, to ask questions we do not yet know to ask, and to expose us to knowledge that already exists but has yet to be discovered. "All creation waits with eager longing for the revealing through the sons of men." (Albert Einstein)[41]

CHAPTER 6

LEARNING IN THE AI AGE

"In times of change, the learners will inherit the earth while the learned find themselves beautifully equipped to deal with a world that no longer exists."

~ERIC HOFFER

Is the education system ready to prepare students for a world running on AI?

In 1965, Dr. Gordon E. Moore, a PhD in chemistry, published a historical article entitled "Cramming More Components onto Integrated Circuits." He saw a pattern in which the number of transistors that would fit on a chip doubled every year. He then extrapolated it on a graphic for the following 10 years and predicted computer chips would double in capacity every two years. This prediction became known as Moore's Law, a vital estimate that offers a good idea of what to expect from the speed of computer and cell phone hardware. In 1967, Moore cofounded

Intel, a company that continues to lead innovation in computer chips. Most likely your computer has an Intel chip inside.

Data and processing capacity are the core of AI. The more data and the faster the ability to process it, the faster lots of information can be analyzed and insights can be at your disposal. I got my first cell phone in 1996. Both the device and the service were very expensive, so I limited its use only to emergencies and business. At that time, I knew by heart the numbers to call all members of my direct and extended family, my friends, and my most important customers. Fast-forward some decades and now mobile hardware and service are extremely affordable. Cell phones do more for us than we could have imagined. Some may affirm that cell phones control their lives. Cell phones call people we want to talk to, suggest products we would most likely buy, find the songs we are in the mood for, calculate distances and give us directions, and so much more. That is the power of AI in our hands and we enjoy living with it, thank you very much.

Take Siri, Apple's voice recognition technology that uses a natural language user interface to help you with everyday tasks, such as scheduling a meeting in your calendar or answering questions. It takes a lot of data processing to identify your voice, interpret what you say, search the internet, and organize the data to present it to you. Apple launched Siri in 2011. Its year-over-year improvement has been notable as this AI system "learns" how people use it, what they use it for, different accents, and so on. The system then cross-references all that data to make itself more efficient every day.

It is a bit challenging for us to conceive what the world will be like a few years from now, as it was challenging to believe in the 1800s that a human could step foot onto the moon. Today, we live in unprecedented times, during which we have witnessed the advent of AI in every industry. So far, this technology has served us well, improving many areas of our lives. How far can we still go?

We can expect AI to evolve exponentially as data accumulation and processing capacity improve and its uses expand. Can you navigate to some unfamiliar place without Waze or Google Maps? I bet you can't. Now, imagine how that could expand in the future: While you're on your way to a meeting, Google Maps gives your self-driving car directions from point A to B and suggests you stop at a natural juice shop for breakfast. Your phone's AI knows you jogged five miles this morning, left home without eating, and have a predicted mood below average because you forgot your wedding anniversary and your wife is mad at you. AI also knows that this shop's ingredient combination is precisely what your DNA requires at this time to have the right amount of energy for your upcoming meeting, according to the data coming from your wearable watch. As you park, Google orders your smoothie and pays with Google Pay before you even enter the store, making your stop less than one minute long. Google plays songs to improve your mood and get you ready for your meeting. This AI knows you better than you know yourself and makes your life very efficient!

The benefits of AI are beyond what our minds can conceive today. Take, for instance, neural interfaces, devices placed inside or outside the brain and interact with the nervous system. They're already used for deep brain stimulation (DBS) in patients with Alzheimer's, Parkinson's, and other movement disorders. Deaf patients use cochlear implants attached to the brain to restore hearing. Transcranial direct current stimulation (tDCS) is used to treat depression, and vagus nerve stimulation is used to treat epilepsy, depression, and addiction. Researchers are now exploring neural interfaces to treat pain, anxiety, and autoimmune disorders.

Researchers are also experimenting with high-density transcranial alternating current stimulation (HD-tACS). The first results on humans demonstrated it sharpens mental skills and alertness, and increases performance in endurance sports, such as cycling. Imagine head-wearables that improve our cognitive skills, make us learn faster and remember more, improve our emotional intelligence, motivate us to exercise and eat well, or allow us to download a new habit, all connected to one single source: the internet. Brain-to-internet interaction at the speed of thought will significantly improve our cognitive power and perhaps enable exponential creativity.

Do you think all of this is crazy? Think again. Entrepreneur Bryan Johnson founded Kernel.co in 2016 to build a "noninvasive mind/body/machine interface (MBMI) to improve, evolve, and extend human cognition." He aims to create the next generation of technologies that can read and write directly from the brain. Elon Musk, founder of electric vehicle pioneer Tesla, founded Neuralink in the same year, with the sole purpose of developing "ultra-high bandwidth brain-machine interfaces to connect humans and computers." In 2018, University of California, Berkeley, presented the world's smallest and most efficient brain implant, "neural dust," a tiny 3-millimeter sensor node that will sit below the cranial dura mater.[42] While previous brain stimulation devices required wired connections even when implanted in the brain, neural dust is wireless, eliminating exposure to infections. Its ultrasound connection to the external world will allow you to share live biometric data directly from your body and stimulate nerves as needed.

These advancements in technology are fascinating. At the same time, they may lead us to overdependence on machines. They will raise questions such as what it is to be human or whether we still have natural cognitive capacities. Moreover, these advances will create ethical issues related to our privacy and autonomy. As it brings benefits, AI also brings challenges. Imagine the exposure of an entire population with implanted neural dust in their brains.

In the past, marketers used subliminal messages to trick our subconscious minds and make us buy certain products. Today, Facebook displays selected feeds on our walls to change our mood, or to offer products specifically related to who we are, what we like, the mood it thinks we're in, and what it thinks we want. And we don't even notice! In the near future, a downloaded virus could reprogram neural dust to store deep new beliefs in our brains. Hackers can already see you through the camera of your computer or TV set. Why wouldn't they read your mind when you use neural devices? If I had neural dust in my brain, how easy would it be for my husband to read my mind when he asks me what is wrong and I answer, "Nothing?" Oh, no, no good, definitively no good! We women will have to reinvent ourselves!

The U.S. alone is responsible for 52.3% of the world's investment in AI, which has grown at an average rate of 56% every year since 2016.[43] During the same period, the K-12 education budget in the U.S. has grown an average rate of 3% per year.[44] Growing investment in AI is a statement that we believe AI is the future. Every day, engineers improve algorithms to make AI more efficient and less costly, while teachers still use an inefficient 19th-century system to make BI work, oblivious to the likelihood that AI will soon surpass BI, and we will have to learn to live with it.

While this future may be scary, these changes are unstoppable. At the pace technology is evolving, the future may well present us with a merger of BI and AI. Transistors perform billions of operations per second with only limited connections to other transistors. The brain's neurons connect to thousands of other neurons at the same time, yet can perform only 1,000 operations per second. We will have incredible brainpower once BI merges with AI, and it will be impossible to give it up. Surely Einstein must be turning in his grave with these possibilities.

Our brains are like a powerful person who is incredibly smart yet unbelievably lazy. The brain is like that by design, to conserve energy. In automatic mode, we are trapped in fast-thinking, I-already-know-this statements, and implicit biases that enable us to reach conclusions as quickly as possible—although not always accurately. Given what the future likely holds for us, we must raise our awareness and pay attention to these brain mechanics and, through cognitive control, make conscious decisions. We must become lifelong learners and develop our emotional intelligence to prepare for what is coming in the near future.

Dr. Jeff Lichtman, a neuroscientist at Harvard University, calculated that indexing the entire human brain would require thousands of zettabytes of data storage. For comparison purposes, the internet is estimated to be 44 zettabytes in 2020. Thus, although we can expect BI and AI to eventually merge, we are still years away from it. We still don't understand our brains' capacity, let alone the power of our consciousness. Neural devices may work with the mechanics of the brain. It's not clear that they'll ever interact with our consciousness.

~ REDEFINING BIOLOGICAL LEARNING FOR THE AGE OF AI ~

What does this mean for education? Learning is our pathway to cognitive control, and consequently, to living well in the era of AI. We must be prepared for the unknown, and we must prepare students for the unknown. Moreover, the people who will be making decisions about the ethical issues that future technologies will raise are sitting in your classrooms right now. Schools must prepare learners to have the right state of mind and the right cognitive awareness to make good decisions. Literally, the future of humanity lies in their hands, and you and I are responsible for paving the way.

So what can we do today to prepare for the future? Technology will certainly continue to advance faster than we think as processing power doubles every year, vast amounts of data are available, and algorithms become increasingly sophisticated. The only tool we have right now as human beings is our brains.

We must first recondition ourselves through learning. Read books, watch videos, participate in conferences, get the brain to work! Most likely, you have heard at your gym that an exercise loses its effect on your muscles if you keep repeating the same workout over and over again. The same thing happens to your brain, which is also a muscle, if you keep repeating what you already know and fail to renew your knowledge. This is why it's important to never, ever stop learning. As transformational speaker Leland Val Van de Wall said, "Learning is when you consciously entertain an idea, get emotionally involved with the idea, step out and act on the idea, and improve the results in some area of your life."

An active learner modifies her behavior with what she has learned. A passive learner memorizes and regurgitates concepts she has never practiced. Because of conditioning through our years of schooling, we are afraid of failing when we introduce concepts to our lives that differ from the status quo. When we learn to take control of the learning process, we can adjust and take control of any situation.

Learning and practicing something new will always take us out of our comfort zone. Thus, as you venture into your next level of learning, you must embrace the growth mindset (see chapter 9). If you want to grow continuously, you must be comfortable with being uncomfortable and with making mistakes. But you must take action; you must make progress. This work will become easier with practice and self-awareness. As you learn, you will be able to inspire others to do the same, finding new meaning in their lives every day.

Isn't it time for us to redefine our biological learning experience? We have a lot to catch up on! AI is evolving at high speed, while BI is falling behind. Educational systems around the world are moving toward more innovative learning approaches with proven results. Our challenge is to make these approaches scalable and adaptable to any context. For the past few decades, researchers have focused on blended learning, project-based learning, competency-based learning, personalized learning, and autonomous learning.

Blended learning combines face-to-face classroom interaction with activities using technology; it fosters some student control, such as in the pacing. In **project-based learning,** students work on a project over a certain period to solve a problem or answer a complex question. Students develop vital skills, such as research, group work, critical thinking, creativity, real-world problem solving, development of an authentic product, and public speaking with the presentation of their project. **Personalized learning** tailors learning to each student's strengths and interests, and gives them a choice and voice in how, when, and where they learn. The possibility of mastery is higher with such flexibility, as students are more interested in exploring new knowledge from their interests. **Competency-based learning** details the pathway to learning specific skills.

Perhaps most relevant of these is **autonomous learning**, in which students have full regulation, control, and responsibility for their learning process. It is a student-centered approach in which learners are aware of their strengths, learning needs, objectives, and cognitive process, and can self-assess their learning through a metacognition process. Autonomous learners are prepared for the AI era because they have full cognitive control, can evoke or ignore thoughts or feelings, and embrace the responsibility to learn rather than relying on a third party to provide them with instructions. We want students to become autonomous learners, and school gives them the opportunity for 16,800 hours of practice at it. Moreover, autonomous learning easily includes most of the innovative learning approaches researched in recent decades.

Dr. Albert Bandura, the Stanford University professor of psychology, has extensively researched self-efficacy, self-regulation, and self-development. He defines autonomy as "the human capability to influence one's functioning and the course of events by one's actions,"[45] or, in other words, having cognitive control.

Bandura identified four practices involved in exercising autonomy:

- **Intentionality**: the practice of a specific intention and a plan to realize it;
- **Forethought**: the practice of setting specific goals to realize the intention, and potential actions to guide and motivate the effort;
- **Self-reactiveness**: the self-regulation to execute the actions; and
- **Self-reflectiveness**: the ability to self-assess one's functioning, to reflect on personal efficacy, the impact of actions, the meaning of pursuits, as well as the ability to perform corrections when needed.

Bandura also defined three forms of agency, which an individual can exercise under their control:

- **Individual agency:** individuals focus on what they can directly control;
- **Proxy agency**: individuals bring into play people who have the resources and knowledge to execute the expected outcome; and
- **Collective agency**: the gathering of knowledge, skills, and resources, and collaboration toward the same goal; must be

exercised by a group of autonomous individuals with high cognitive control.

The framework shared in this book fosters the development of these three forms of agency with a doable and straightforward six-step learning process that you can use today.

The vast majority of learners around the world grow up with the mindset of trying to get things done as quickly as possible and fulfilling the minimum requirements so they can be done with school and enter a profession. AI is replacing most of the jobs we know, and performing them significantly better than us. So what is left for human beings? We must wake up and get ready to enable children to create the world around us, regardless of the pathway they choose for their future. And we must foster nonhackable beings. The only way to do this is by developing cognitive awareness through learning, which will ultimately result in cognitive control. In other words, we must learn to use our brains effectively.

Will AI ever replace educators? Though AI is growing and will continue to grow significantly, there has not been an advancement in computer consciousness. Even if computers were to gain their own form of consciousness, our human consciousness has a stronger power, one that we don't yet completely understand. While AI may replace repetitive tasks educators perform, it will likely never replace the human connection.

The brain interprets basic information from someone's facial expressions in just 33 milliseconds, and it immediately reacts to it. Dr. David Eagleman, a neuroscience professor at Stanford University, measured these tiny facial expressions through an experiment where he recorded people's reactions to pictures of faces, some frowning, some smiling, some crying, and so on. Participants mirrored the same facial expressions of the images they saw. Why? Our brains are wired to connect and influence other human beings. Therefore, if we have good or bad habits, if we are happy or sad, or if we are joyful or have addictions, we will influence others to do the same. That is our human connection.

On a separate note, Eagleman's research also found that people who have received Botox injections are less likely to relate to others. This neurotoxin inhibits facial expressions, and an individual's inability to make certain expressions impairs their ability to recognize emotions on someone else's face, and thus, connect to that person. The brain helps us relate to others by mirroring their facial expressions without us even noticing!

~ KEEPING HUMANS RELEVANT IN AN AI WORLD ~

While the human brain will continue to have capabilities that AI cannot begin to touch, our existence will nonetheless be redefined with the Superintelligence Singularity, which refers to a time when AI surpasses humans' biological intelligence. Scientists say it will happen before 2030. If AI is doing all that humans did before, with higher capacity, precision, and quality, two things may happen: We may thrive, discovering the full extent of the capacity of consciousness and entering a period of unimaginable creation and discovery. Or we may be condemned to live in falsehood inside virtual worlds created by ourselves or by AI. It is time to get ready for this rapidly approaching future.

Perhaps the next significant human evolution is the discovery that our brains are underutilized, and we will use our education practices to explore our maximum potential. The world of AI is highly personalized to each user, and so should learning be in this new normal. We can then uncover every human talent, making this world a better place to live.

To personalize learning means to become a catalyst for students' learning experiences. According to Dictionary.com, catalysis means "an action between two or more persons or forces, initiated by an agent [teacher, parent, business leader, coach, and so on] that itself remains unaffected by the action." In this usage, it means learners initiate learning and have the initiative to move forward. Personalized learning means coaching learners to discover their passions and guiding them toward developing the necessary knowledge and skills to excel in those passions. Autonomous learning will prepare learners to continue to foster their skills for life.

Think of each learner as a seed in your hands. Your work is to plant it and take care of it, so it flourishes. The seed will grow according to what it is inside. In other words, an apple seed will give you apples, not orchids just because you want it to. Thus, let us refrain from telling learners what to be, and start supporting and guiding them to flourish with what they have inside, their passion. Our starting point is an individual full of potential just waiting to be realized, rather than just a blank page.

~ IDENTIFY YOUR CURRENT TEACHING PRACTICES—THE COMPASS ASSESSMENT ~

I personally believe AI will bring us great advancements to improve our lives. I also believe we are in a pivotal moment for humankind's future, where we have the chance to move the needle toward more meaningful learning, and to equip students to coexist with AI and lead in this new normal. Our inaction may continue to result in underdeveloped cognitive and socioemotional skills for students, opening the gates for AI's power to eliminate the need for us to think! What would be the meaning of our existence if that happens?

This is not a war between AI and BI. As a matter of fact, we have no choice, as AI is here to stay. Instead, I am making a case to prepare learners to augment their cognitive abilities and apply them for the benefit of humankind. Well-prepared students will create the next generation of AI algorithms and decide on policies that will impact everyone's lives. You do not have control over AI, so work on what you do control: your own learning and your students' learning. Where should you start? It is simple: from where you are.

Earlier in this chapter, we covered a variety of learning approaches. So which is the best approach? Learning models can complement each other and benefit the learner. Some educators practice one model more predominantly than others do. However, even if, for example, you believe you are purely a project-based educator, you may well be practicing other models in certain dimensions.

The Compass Assessment is a comprehensive, free tool that will help you identify where you are with your current teaching practices and help guide you on a more effective professional development journey. The Compass Assessment breaks down education practices into seven main dimensions, based on the learning-innovation research, development, and implementation we have done at Learning One to One. It consists of a series of questions to identify where an educator's practice concentrates the most, and provides a personalized report with a recommended professional development pathway for continuous improvement.

~ THE SEVEN MAIN DIMENSIONS OF EDUCATION PRACTICE ~

- **Organization**: management of physical spaces and learning pace;
- **Methodology**: student-educator relationship and the educator's role;
- **Flexibility**: malleability of objectives, calendar, and academic curriculum and content;
- **Intellectual Process**: development of students' cognitive skills;

- **Socioemotional Process**: development of students' socio-emotional skills;
- **Assessment**: objectives and tools to assess learning; and
- **Learning Community**: organizational and relational structure of the education institution.

~ THE COMPASS ASSESSMENT'S FUNCTIONS ~

- A **self-awareness tool**, allowing educators to reflect on their current practices;
- A **guiding tool** to define professional development needs and help educators effectively engage in professional growth; and
- An **entryway** to a personalized professional development plan.

You can access the Compass Assessment at BecomingEinsteinsTeacher.com.

Educators greatly influence students' development and life journeys; thus, it is important to invest in continuous professional development for those whose profession is to form future generations. Use the Compass Assessment to learn where your practices are mostly focused and discover your optimal professional development pathway.

Although the U.S. investment in education grows very slowly year after year, it is still higher than in many other countries. So, we have the opportunity to make smarter decisions on the use of available resources. In other words, we can make the system more efficient to achieve better results. Companies do that all the time to serve their customers better. What would it take for us to do the same in education?

CHAPTER 7

WHO REPLACED MOZART?

"We are what we repeatedly do. Excellence,
therefore, is not an action but a habit."

~**Aristotle**

In previous chapters, we explored the need to never stop learning in order to evolve our biological intelligence continuously. We also discussed how the traditional way of teaching and learning suppresses motivation. What should we do to enable students to enjoy a lifelong learning experience? What is the one thing that can get them emotionally involved with what they learn, move them to act on it, and improve many areas of their lives?

Two centuries ago, Wolfgang Amadeus Mozart (1756–1791) was paying close attention to the music lessons his father, Leopold, provided to his 7-year-old sister, Maria Anna Mozart. Young Wolfgang Mozart was only 3 years old, living with his family in a small apartment in Salzburg,

Austria. The size of the place did not matter much, but the many instruments to play, available around the house, mattered greatly. He was delighted to hear how good his piano sounded whenever he touched it.

The music lessons continued daily and by the age of 5 Mozart had composed his first piece of music. His composition signature was noticeable from the beginning: His creations followed the steps of contemporary composers, with a touch of innovation in between the notes, making them distinguishably unique. His music had personality, what many still call "genius." Mozart's father never had to force the boy to practice. Young Wolfgang had the self-motivation to keep practicing, composing, and performing.

Leopold Mozart took his son all over Europe, exposing him to high society and musicians of the time. Mozart, having discovered his love for music at a young age, nurtured this love throughout his life. He knew what he was capable of and was determined to live his life doing what he loved. Mozart worked for who he wanted and composed what pleased him and his audience.[46]

At the age of 25, Mozart wrote in a letter to his father: "My main goal right now is to meet the emperor in some agreeable fashion, I am absolutely determined he should get to know me. I would be so happy if I could whip through my opera for him and then play a fugue or two, for that's what he likes."[47] The Austrian emperor, Joseph II, did meet the young musician and supported his career substantially for many years to come. Mozart never settled for less than what he was capable of, and always sought to improve in each new composition.[48] He was an inspiration for many composers after him, including Ludwig van Beethoven (1770–1827), Pyotr Ilyich Tchaikovsky (1840–1893), and Fryderyk Franciszek Chopin (1810–1849).

What we experience nowadays is very different from Mozart's determination, creativity, and motivation. Try this: Go to LinkedIn and check the profiles of some of your connections. I bet most of them will enumerate functions performed in different organizations, but not necessarily what makes them unique. "Managed this, responsible for that," they will show. This is just a consequence of the factory-like education we received: We learned that we have a role and we are replaceable because the focus is on the task instead of the person's uniqueness.

If Mozart lived today, his LinkedIn profile would read something like this: My name is Wolfgang Amadè Mozart. I am a distinguished professional musician and composer of classical music. What makes me different from other composers is my ability to write award-winning pieces in every major classical genre with advanced technical sophistication and emotional reach. I play the piano, violin, harpsichord, and clavier. I have composed over 600 symphonies, concertos, and operas so far, among them *The Paris Symphony*, *The Marriage of Figaro*, *Don Giovanni*, *Haydn Quartets*, and *The Magic Flute*. Do you feel goosebumps when you listen to my creations? That is me! It is the emotion I invest in each of my compositions. It moves from my heart directly to yours. I am currently working on *Requiem in D Minor*. I have also performed throughout Europe for princes, emperors, and members of the court. I have been composing since I was 5 years old, with the guidance of my beloved father and the support of my mother and sister. Today, my two sons and wife are my inspiration to continue composing and performing, along with my infinite love of music. I am available for commissions; Please email me to inquire about my work.

In truth, while most companies talk about finding, developing, and keeping talent, they compartmentalize talent within a function. Therefore, once someone leaves, they find a new person to replace them and perform the required work. After all, the function remains the same. It is just a matter of performing specific tasks within a particular function, as in a factory. In my 20-plus years of working for Fortune

100 corporations, I learned no one is irreplaceable in functional work. Reflect on this: Are we educating today's students for functional work or to best express and utilize their own unique talents?

Wolfgang Amadeus Mozart. Marie Curie. Henry Ford. Florence Griffith "Flo-Jo" Joyner. Abraham Lincoln. Thomas Edison. Albert Einstein. Amelia Earhart. Nikola Tesla. Aretha Franklin. These individuals—and many others—left their marks on the world in unique ways. There might be other musicians, inventors, mathematicians, or athletes who will be remembered by their own legacies, not in the same way as these individuals. How can we make this the norm?

~ INTRINSIC MOTIVATION—THE FORCE BEHIND MAKING A MARK ~

We have little idea of what it takes to become an Olympic gold medalist, or create a new industry, or make a difference as a community leader. We only know the outcomes: the beautiful songs, the emotions on the winning athlete's face, the improved communities, the results of developed potential. We know that each of these individuals had an intrinsic motivation that kept them going regardless of what other people said or the circumstances in which they lived—because they loved what they were doing. Because of this intrinsic motivation, each of them was able to unlock their potential, realize their dreams, and thrive in their lives.

In education, we talk about potential all the time. What does "potential" mean? In our definition, it is the combination of skills that makes a person unique and unlocks their infinite value. Each of us has our own unique potential that only we can develop. What we need to learn is how to unleash it. An educator's job is to accelerate the process of fostering each learner's full potential. To do this, we must build their intrinsic motivation so they do the work to get there.[49] This is precisely the opposite of what most learners experience in today's schools.

Let's look at some of the elements of intrinsic motivation and their importance in helping individuals reach their potential. Here's an example: In 2010, skier Lindsey Vonn won the International Ski Federation (FIS) Alpine Ski World Cup in women's downhill. In an interview, she admitted to making a "big mistake" on the first part of the course, and fans doubted she could win. "I just kept fighting the whole way down," she said. "My skiing wasn't perfect today, but it was set in the right direction." She focused her attention on her journey and won by 0.68 of a second. Vonn's performance is also a good reminder that performing up to potential does not necessarily mean perfect execution, but knowing you have the ability to correct course and achieve the desired result.

Intrinsic motivation is that internal force that motivates us to do something when we know there will be a meaningful, valuable reward, such as pursuing our passion, enjoying a task, or upholding a moral value. Intrinsic motivation fosters a personal desire to do and be better. This state maintains a nice balance of dopamine and endorphins. In contrast, extrinsic motivation drives a specific behavior with an external reward, such as money, a voucher, or goods. In the case of the education system, the external reason is mainly good grades and what they can lead to. It creates a brain state with an extra dose of norepinephrine neurotransmitters with extreme protection and little room to experience failure. Intrinsic motivation is what keeps athletes training, entrepreneurs working, musicians composing, and scientists researching. While some people are naturally more inclined to have intrinsic motivation than others, researchers now understand it is a skill that can be developed.[50]

~ DEVELOPING INTRINSIC MOTIVATION ~

When people are intrinsically motivated, they perform better and have higher personal satisfaction, as Daniel Pink, *New York Times* best-selling author, shows in his many books on business success.[51] People who are intrinsically motivated understand that effort brings the rewards they want. The prerequisite to developing intrinsic motivation is "believing we have authority over our actions and surroundings," Pulitzer prize-winning reporter and science writer Charles Duhigg wrote in his book *Smarter Faster Better*.[52] "Motivation is triggered by making choices that demonstrate to ourselves that we are in control. The specific choice we make matters less than the assertion of control. It's this feeling of self-determination that gets us going." In other words, intrinsic motivation requires autonomy: being self-directed, the ability to make our own decisions.

Duhigg also wrote in that same book about the research of Columbia University psychologists, published in the journal *Trends in Cognitive Sciences* in 2010. "**The need for control is a biological imperative**," he quoted from their work, then wrote, "When people believe they are in control, research shows that they work harder, are more resilient, and push themselves more. Each choice—no matter how small—reinforces the perception of control and self-efficacy." To help learners develop intrinsic motivation, we must deliberately empower them to plan, take action, make decisions, change their course of action, and transform themselves. We must guide them to become autonomous learners.[53]

It's amazing the way even preteen students behave when they are empowered in this way. A few years ago, I visited a school in Mexico whose teachers received continuous professional development from my organization, focusing on understanding and imparting learning autonomy. I noticed two 11-year-old students, Ana and Nicolas, studying math. "What are you doing?" I asked. "I am helping Nicolas with math," Ana answered. "Why are you doing that?" I replied. "Well, because I am way advanced and he is behind, and he asked for my help," Ana answered back. "Nicolas, why are you behind?" I asked. "I decided to play and got behind in math." "Hum . . . and what will you do differently next time?" I inquired. "I will plan my time better next time: time to play and time to learn math," Nicolas replied. Notice Nicolas never said he had difficulty learning math or dislikes math. He understood it was a matter of planning his time better to get the job done. In this school, learners themselves incorporate the belief that they can do whatever they set their minds to.

Having control of their learning motivates learners to achieve mastery, an "I-can-do-this" attitude. In this journey to get better at something, learners develop key skills that will serve them for life, including resilience. Interestingly, one of the main factors researchers found in increased resilience is the degree of control someone has over their situation and their ability to identify and use their skills to change the situation. As students' autonomy increases, their mastery increases, and this leads to even stronger intrinsic motivation. Add in a purpose, and students will be highly motivated and happy. The journey is no longer a pain when learners have designed their own destination!

Jonathan, a 13-year-old, helps his parents harvest coffee in Concordia, Colombia, from October to December. The school year runs from January to November there, and at his age, he would normally have to drop out of school because his work impedes him from attending the final two months. However, Jonathan's parents learned about a school in Itagui, a town two hours away from where they live, that provides a new learning framework that allows Jonathan to stay in school. In this school, Jonathan is responsible for his own learning. He knows he must finish one full grade by the end of September, two months before the school year ends, so he can harvest coffee with his family and still invest in his future by attending school. He still must reach 100% of attainment to move to the next grade. Because he has learned there are opportunities ahead of him beyond harvesting coffee and he has been empowered with learning autonomy, Jonathan has an intrinsic motivation to learn, nurtured by his autonomy, mastery of the learning process, and sense of purpose. He is fully committed to completing his work by September each year.

The good news is that there is plenty of scientific research proving intrinsic motivation can be developed at any age. Our own practice with schools has proved it over and over. As students achieve small successes, confidence and self-esteem increase. They start believing in their personal capabilities and their ability to succeed at a task.[53] It is their intrinsic motivation that drives them to dive into learning. We found that it is easier to foster learners' potential than to fix their deficiencies and try to adapt them to the education system! I'll share with you the details on how to foster intrinsic motivation, learning autonomy, and mastery in your students in further chapters.

~ THE VALUE OF FAILURE ~

Life is full of successes and failures. Every individual mentioned in this chapter had failures before making the history they became known for. They succeeded because of intrinsic motivation. How did they deal with failure?

Failure is a crucial part of autonomous learning. Think of the process of a child learning to walk: crawl, stumble, stay up, stumble again, take a couple of steps, fall, and finally walk. We must follow the same process with learners: allow them to stumble, fall, and achieve mastery by themselves in all aspects of their lives. Failure in the safety of the school environment and with the support of their teachers will help learners to improve their skills, correct course, and keep growing.

Take this story from my own life: When I was 5 years old, I discovered the *Wonder Woman* TV series. She was a beautiful woman, well dressed, always with her hair neatly up. Whenever she had the chance to help others, she would transform into Wonder Woman by turning around in a circle, which invoked a bright light that would give her wavy hair, a special outfit, and superpowers. I was just amazed how this woman fought bad people, jumped from buildings, flew an invisible plane, and stopped bullets with her golden bracelets.

One inspiring day I was playing outside, impersonating Wonder Woman, and decided to jump from a tree. At that time, TV programs did not have a do-not-try-this-at-home disclaimer. So I believed my superpowers would make me land perfectly, just like Wonder Woman! After all, I was a female, too, and therefore, entitled to the same superpowers. However, it turned out that was not the case. I broke my front tooth and got various bruises. My front tooth was not replaced for two years, reminding me I should avoid jumping from trees and I was not Wonder Woman. It was disappointing, but a lesson learned for life.

My mother could have helped me to never have that experience and avoid breaking my tooth just by prohibiting me from climbing and jumping from trees. However, if she had done so, I would have never been able to reach my own conclusions about what I am capable of or identify which skills I need to perform specific tasks, all in the safety of my family environment. I carried this practice into my work as a leader and manager, allowing members of my team to try their ideas, fail if necessary, and reach their own conclusions about whether the ideas were good or needed improvement.

Education must be about helping children to write their own histories. Setbacks will develop resilience, so let them try and fail as many times as necessary in the safety of the school environment. What is the consequence of making a mistake? The only reference children have today is video games, where they have seven lives and live again after someone "kills" them. That's actually a pretty useful reference.

The more we are aware of and practice overcoming obstacles, the more we are prepared to face them. The power of perspective—in this case, reaching a higher goal—can change the way we deal with setbacks, and we can help learners identify this power while they are in school. They will end up learning that it is good to have resistance because it is a sign of moving forward! After all, airplanes take off against the wind. In biological terms, we form neural networks to deal with any obstacle we face, as Lindsey Vonn did in the first part of the Alpine Skiing World Cup course, when she made a mistake but trusted she could still finish with a personal best time.

We think that successful people have superpowers. However, in reality, they have discovered the combination of skills that makes them successful—a power that is available to everyone. Our job as educators, parents, and leaders is to give learners the right tools to feed their intrinsic motivation through the belief they can achieve what they desire, and reach success on their own terms. After all, the word education comes from the Latin word *educare*, which means "to draw out, to develop from within, to bring forth from within."

~ KEEPING BRAINS IN MOTION ~

In summary, every time your students have small successes, their intrinsic motivation increases, and so does the belief they can accomplish whatever goals they set for themselves. Learners will aim higher and higher as you challenge them. It is dopamine at work in their brains. So, how do we get this cycle of intrinsic motivation and small success achievement going? We keep students' brains working.

Newton's first law of motion says that objects at rest tend to stay at rest, and objects in motion tend to stay in motion, unless acted upon by an outside force. So what happens within our industrial-era school system, that keeps students' brains nearly at rest, receiving information until they graduate from high school, attend college, and only then put their brains to work? If it takes 10,000 hours of practice to become an expert on anything and students spend 16,800 hours—kindergarten through high school—practicing to sit and wait for the next instruction, what can we expect from these students in adulthood? I believe students' brains are at rest during their K-12 journey, and, having had so much practice in this state, will tend to stay at rest once they graduate. No wonder companies complain that younger employees lack initiative and interpersonal skills. It happened to me! Remember my send-a-proposal-via-fax story from chapter 4?

What does it mean for the brain to stay at rest in the work world? Take this example: Two well-paid, well-educated engineers once shared with me that most projects they are involved in can be completed in hours, but they convince their managers they will take three to seven days. These engineers shared that this is how they keep their jobs—by convincing their managers that their challenging contributions take a lot of time. Most likely, their managers work in a similar fashion. I believe this attitude comes from 16,800 hours of practice at school, during which people learn that they need only to do passable work, rather than excellent work. When brains get used to being at rest, people only perform the function they were hired to do. They don't innovate, so the world loses productivity and new ideas.

Let me share a story from a trip to Argentina several years ago. During the taxi ride from the airport to my hotel, Matias, my driver, complained about the unimpressive administration of the new president and how the economy was suffering. He surprised me, though, when he identified education as the most critical issue to solve in his country, and that a better education system would allow Argentina "to have productive and respectful citizens." "If I could fix the education system," he continued,

"I'd make sure students learn to persevere. I am 56 years old and a taxi driver. I started so many projects and never finished them . . . I could be in a much better place today if my teachers would have helped me work on my potential and if I had learned to persevere."

Matias is a product of an education system that requires students to do exactly as they are told, following someone else's definition of success, and receiving recognition only from the person who defined success. After so many years, the brain gets used to this very specific training: "Do what I say and be rewarded with the grade that only I can give you." Now you understand why Matias could never finish his personal projects. Although he tried hard to set goals for himself, he was used to seeking recognition and approval from others. The very first negative feedback from anyone was enough for him to give up! Matias may have been talented in something, but without acting on it, his talent became irrelevant. Talent is not about having skills, but about having the ability to develop them.

Matias is right to say education should be addressing the issue he faced his entire life. Research demonstrates that students CAN develop perseverance at school through exposure to situations where they can practice resilience in the face of adversity or hardship.[54] Perseverance is a consequence of intrinsic motivation. The safe school environment allows appropriate coaching to identify, cope with, adapt to, and recover from adversity. Perseverance develops resilience, which equips learners to pursue and realize their full potential.

Humans can and should grow to their full potential—everything else in nature does so, unless it's moved off course. A tree grows to its highest height. A tiger is as strong as it can be. Mountains around the world continue to grow. You have never seen a small adult elephant. How many 56-year-olds do you know in the same situation as Matias, never able to grow to their potential? Humans are the only ones who limit their own potential!

When people of any age are encouraged to rev up their brains, they feel motivated and engaged. No parent, teacher, company, or country wants individuals depending on them all their lives. Yet industrial school systems, by keeping students' brains at rest, are creating this dependency. On the other hand, if we keep students' brains "moving" during school they will continue to move once they leave school.

Companies like Uber and Airbnb became a great success in recent years, operating on business models that tap into underutilized resources, such as a car in the garage or a temporarily vacant house. Now think of the things students could do if school systems made better use of their underutilized brains, allowing them to "move" more often in the safety of the school environment. They would have the opportunity to practice and become experts on the things they are passionate about: inventions, solutions, techniques, sports, and so much more! After their 16,800 hours of "brain in motion" practice, their brains would tend to stay in motion for the rest of their lives. "Life is like riding a bicycle. To stay balanced you must keep moving." (Albert Einstein)

The question in the title of this chapter is a trick one. Joseph Haydn, an Austrian composer of the Classical period, wrote of Mozart: "Posterity will not see such a talent again in 100 years."[55] He was wrong. Posterity will not see a talent like Mozart again at all. No one replaced Mozart, and no one will. Each human being has a unique talent to contribute to the world. Each of us is the only one who truly understands our own unique potential and how to nurture it. And, while talent allows one to improve particular skills more quickly, it is the continuous *effort* to practice that makes those skills productive and useful. That's why it so important for the education system to develop each student's intrinsic motivation and learning autonomy, consequently fostering their potential.

If every person could impact the world in as unique a way as Mozart did, we would definitely be a more advanced society. An undeveloped talent is just a potential-to-be talent, an unexpressed potential. What will be your students' stories 200 years from now?

You already know what it takes to help them live fantastic stories: intrinsic motivation. So, where do you start? You can begin by transforming your own practices as an educator, a parent, or a leader. Follow the advice of Roman philosopher Marcus Aurelius: "Waste no more time arguing about what a good man should be. Be one." Learn how in the next chapters.

CHAPTER 8

THE INFINITE GAME

"Amateurs practice until they get it right.
Professionals practice until they can't get it wrong."

–Peter Voogd

The movie *Free Solo* is a documentary about Alex Honnold's attempt to climb the 3,300-foot (1,006-meter) granite face of El Capitán, in California's Yosemite National Park, without ropes. In it, Alex, then 32, shared how he practiced obsessively to execute the climb. First he practiced with ropes, trying grips and steps in different parts of El Capitán, assessing what worked and what didn't, trying again, assessing, and so on, until he knew what would work. Then, he repeated the best route over, and over, and over again, assessing his performance after each practice, perfecting moves, until he knew what worked best. His mind and body were used to the climb and he could remember exactly the next step.

In biological terms, through his practice, self-assessment, and further practice, Honnold was strengthening his climb-El-Capitán-with-no-ropes neural network until the skill was stored in his cerebellum and he could do it without thinking twice.

Honnold knew he had to be physically and mentally prepared. After all, three people had died in previous attempts at the ropeless climb. If he could make it, he would be the first one to do so. He knew that one wrong grip or one slip would mean the end of his life. During the two-year preparation, Honnold hurt himself many times, had doubts, felt the burden. Many of his self-assessments showed things he needed to improve. The magnitude of the goal sometimes scared him. To make things worse, people around him pressured him hard to make it happen fast, which took an emotional toll.

On June 3, 2017, Alex Honnold climbed the 3,300-foot face of El Capitán without ropes or any other safety gear, in three hours and 56 minutes. For comparison purposes, the average climber takes three to five days to climb the 0.6-mile high El Capitán with ropes. Yes, it means having to sleep a couple of nights hanging on the wall.

"It is all about performance," Honnold said in the documentary. "Nobody achieves anything great because they are happy. It is about being a warrior. It doesn't matter the cause—this is your path and you will pursue it with excellence. You face your fear because your cause demands it." In his pursuit of excellence, Honnold became the first athlete to push rock climbing to its highest limits of physical skill, risk-taking, and mental strength. This is the same resilience and relentless attitude cultivated by the entrepreneur founding a multibillion-dollar company in their parents' garage or the scientist working on the next significant discovery.

This story demonstrates several lessons relevant to effective learning:

1. Self-assessment is crucial in mastering a skill—or a mountain.

2. Great achievements come only through the pursuit of excellence—and this pursuit must be continuous.

3. Each individual has a personal excellence level they should strive to reach—we can't all learn to free-climb El Capitán, but we can each pursue our own best performance.

People admire heroes like Honnold—human beings who do the impossible, who believe they can do whatever they set their minds to. Have you noticed how motivated you get to conquer the world after watching an inspiring movie? The blockbuster movies are the ones where good wins, love prevails, ordinary people overcome life-threatening challenges, and heroes end evil.

Avengers: End Game, for instance, opened for presale on April 2, 2019, and crashed all websites selling tickets for the April 26 release. The film was expected to generate over $800 million during its opening weekend alone, but topped $1.2 billion. The same people buying those tickets are sitting in your classroom or working in your office, yearning to have a life full of adventures where they can be the winners. People have a craving to believe in something, to be challenged, to find in their core the intensity that will bring purpose to their lives. They want to get involved in the pursuit of something bigger than themselves, something worthy. They want to be the Alex Honnold of their own story.

As a teacher, you can tap into this desire to help your students pursue their own excellence. Guide them to become the heroes in their own lives by showing them life can be an infinite game.

~ WHAT IS AN INFINITE GAME? ~

"There are at least two kinds of games. One could be called finite; the other infinite," philosopher James P. Carse wrote in his book *Finite and*

Infinite Games: A Vision of Life as Play and Possibility. Finite games, he explained, have clear rules known by all players, and end when a single player wins. Because a finite game must have a winner, there is a huge focus on enforcing the rules to maintain the "fairness" to all players. Card games, sports, and many board games and video games are finite. Players compete against each other. Someone must win, and the rest of the players must lose.

An infinite game's objective, on the other hand, is never to end. Rules, boundaries, and even players may change along the way to keep the game alive. In Carse's definition: "finite players play within boundaries; infinite players play with boundaries." In infinite games, players contribute to keeping the game alive with a clear purpose. Players have continuous awareness, able to identify the required resources and skills they need to develop. There are no losers; everyone is a winner as long as the game continues. The challenge is to keep the game alive.

Infinite games are an integral part of our lives. It is hard to know what will happen in the future when we choose a particular career, get married, have kids, change jobs, move to a new country, and so on. Big decisions in life are make-it-or-break-it once choices are made. We can never go back and undo the choices, but must continue to play the infinite game before us.

~ THE FINITE GAME OF STANDARDIZED TESTS ~

Standardized tests evaluate students' capacity to remember—or memorize—what they have, in theory, learned throughout the school year. They create a dynamic of competition because their nature is to compare one student's testing performance to another's under the same set of rules, and give those students A to F labels: winners and losers. This culture becomes prominent throughout learners' lives: Striving to be "the best" gets in the way of being better than they were yesterday. Like finite games, standardized tests require rules set by a third party—the education system—and compare students to each other. The students end up frustrated when they do not win.

In 2014, Katie Brown from Seattle, Washington, was named Washington State Teacher of the Year. When Bill Gates interviewed her, she shared a big disappointment she had grappled with: She had a student who arrived from another country and advanced four grade levels in English in just one year, after "heroic work from him and his teachers." And yet, his scores on standardized tests said he was not proficient in his grade level. How frustrating is that for the student and his family? What is the likelihood of him dropping out? How does this impact his self-esteem?

I have met many teachers who, like this teacher of the year, are frustrated when their students' assessments do not reflect or evaluate the *effort* students put in. Standardized tests create a fear-based culture for students and educators. Students learn that if they don't sit quietly, pay attention, do their homework, and do well on tests, they will be nobody in life. Educators learn that if their students don't do well on tests, they don't get a salary bonus or may even have resources taken away. What kind of world are we preparing students for? One where they must follow orders or be penalized?

"Experts" use standardized test results to define what potential we have or what we are capable of. When learners receive low scores on these measures, they may give up because these "experts" tell them they cannot perform to the standard; many will spend the rest of their lives believing they are, therefore, incapable. Because the result of their efforts is either unpleasant or insufficiently rewarding, their brain doesn't produce dopamine. This lack of dopamine discourages learners from continuing to try. They often end up blaming outside influences for their failure: teachers, their school, their socioeconomic conditions, a lack of technology or labs, or any variety of factors. When students aren't taught to assume responsibility for their own learning and actions, they believe they are incapable of changing their life situation.

The "experts" considered many successful people who changed the world a failure. Einstein, Edison, and Leonardo da Vinci would probably be diagnosed by today's school system as having ADHD and be given drugs to "fix" it. They did not fit the norm. Young Leo asked too many questions, Albert was told "he'd never amount to anything," and little Thomas was labeled by one of his teachers as "unable to think clearly."

Despite having only three months of schooling, Edison became the greatest American inventor. Who believed in him and motivated him to explore his potential? His mother, Nancy Edison, who offered encouragement, confidence, high standards, and a "superb education in learning how to learn," according to the book *Innovate Like Edison*.[56] Little Thomas was lucky to have a mother like Nancy, a natural educator. By the way, Edison lost most of his hearing while still a child, but it was never an impediment to his success.

~ THE REAL WORLD OF THE INFINITE GAME ~

In the real world, many companies are thriving by playing an infinite game, rather than a finite one. Rather than focusing on competition and obsessing about making each quarter's numbers, these companies focus on their mission and purpose first. This includes Costco, which ignores Wall Street expectations and profit-margin demands to instead focus on continuously building a company that will be around for the next 20 years. At Apple, the late Steve Jobs helped rescue the company by refocusing it on the finest device innovations and transforming the way we use technology.

What kind of human beings do we want to form in schools? If we teach students to play an infinite game, they will learn the habit of always transforming themselves, which is a key to happiness in this ever-changing world. Continuous self-improvement creates inner peace, and, therefore, a better quality of life. And, putting educators into an infinite game instead of a finite one will lead to happier educators, focused on innovation and finding new ways to bring out the best in each individual learner.

Children CAN learn to play the infinite game of life with appropriate practice while in a safe school environment. By allowing learners to choose a path and experience the consequences of their choice, we also allow them to gain awareness of how decisions impact their reality. This practice will prepare them to avoid a lifetime of regrets like Matias, the 56-year-old taxi driver I wrote about in chapter 7. Andres, Ana, Nicolas, and Jonathan are having an entirely different life experience, as they practiced designing their futures from an early age. Adults can also learn to play the infinite game of life by developing self-awareness, understanding clearly what they want from life, and forming a plan to get there. Each of us has stories to tell about lessons learned throughout our adult lives, the infinite game we have been playing all along.

Fortunately, the education community around the world believes that student-centered education—an infinite-game-style approach—is the next evolution in the field. We must step forward and introduce scalable personalized assessments in which students can evaluate where they are today versus where they were yesterday, and continue to evolve. This will carry them beyond their time in school. A 21st-century assessment looks like an infinite game in which students are continually striving to be better than themselves. There is no focus on competition or comparison to others, but rather, the focus is on one's continuous self-improvement to benefit oneself and the community.

The 21st-century assessment:

1. **Respects differences with personalized assessments.**

   Each person is unique and can bring significant value to the world. When we focus on each student's strengths instead of solely on their weaknesses, we improve their self-esteem, intrinsic motivation, and resilience so they continue to thrive. Failure is part of the learning process and will never define those who know they can learn.

2. **Recognizes each student's personal excellence level.**

   The 21st-century assessment is personalized to each student and helps them to reach their own excellence level. Think of excellence as progress, not perfection. Gold-medal-winning athletes practice being better than themselves, not being better than others. That is the story of Flo-Jo, Michael Phelps, and Lindsey Vonn. They set their own bar for excellence, enjoy the journey, and are awarded the results. At my organization, we have seen how reaching excellence in everything students do has a positive effect that goes well beyond school. Parents tell us that their children become better "citizens" of the house—for example, taking charge of household chores. I believe the practice of giving their best at school translates into giving their best in relationships, careers, community involvement, and more.

3. **Shifts to constant quality and variable time.**

   In today's education, time is constant and quality is variable. At the end of the school year (time), students end up with As, Cs, Fs, or any other standardized qualification (variable). Much attention is paid to standardized tests to measure how one student compares to another, but we need to ask some hard questions: Are tests helping children pursue their dreams? What if we shifted to education where quality is constant and time is variable? The primary measurement of success would become the effort that students apply to reach each milestone of excellence, regardless of how long it takes to get there. Some children learn to walk in 9 months, and others walk in 14 months. What matters is that all of them walk, regardless of the time it takes to learn.

So does it mean that every student will be an "A" student? In our minds, we associate excellence with "A," and this should not be the case. Each individual has their own excellence level. And that is why it's time to exclude letter grades from our vocabulary when it comes to education. This can be done while still complying with curriculum requirements. Assessment is personalized to learners, and each reaches their own excellent level. After all, we never hear about *quantity* of life—getting an "A" life compared to someone else's. But we do talk frequently about *quality* of life—having an extraordinary life.

4. **Develops each person's ability to perform conscious self-assessment—the metacognition process.**

We are always assessing everything around us. Right now, you are evaluating whether these ideas make sense to you or not. Perhaps you are thinking of dinner tonight, who is supposed to pick up the kids after soccer practice, or the report you will share at your meeting tomorrow. These assessments allow us to make decisions, whether minor or more significant. The conscious assessment is a process that will enable us to learn, to make decisions, to self-improve, to be self-critical, to be self-directed, and so many other benefits that create a better life experience. Self-assessment widens our vision: We move from asking, *Why* can't I do this, to asking, *How* do I do this? That was what Alex Honnold did every step of the way until he summited El Capitán; or Thomas Edison, who went through thousands of theories and many failed experiments before he invented the lightbulb.[57] We move from "thinking" we can do or be, to "knowing" we can do and be.

5. **Gives learners the freedom to demonstrate learning.**

Whenever students can relate what they learned to what they love, it will be easier to demonstrate learning. It is like trying to speak a new language and engaging in a conversation. It is so much easier to talk about what you love and what inspires you! In a recent school visit, a student shared with me that he learned limits in math and related it to his passion, enumerating various psychology and philosophy authors who discussed how human beings limit themselves. He loves literature and wants to be a psychologist.

After climbing El Capitán, Honnold shared that he felt a sense of calm and freedom while going up. It is his definition of being "high," which, biologically speaking, means a nice dose of dopamine and endorphins unfolding throughout the entire body. Honnold's continuous practice and self-assessment inhibited large amounts of adrenaline, which would cause stress, and norepinephrine, which would make his body get ready for a "fight or flight" response, during his actual climb. Any unbalance of norepinephrine or epinephrine, and Honnold would be dead.

The 21st-century assessment develops an ongoing capacity for continuous self-improvement, keeping alive the infinite game of living an outstanding life. If learners are practicing it for 16,800 hours in their school years, they will do the unimaginable in life, like Alex Honnold.

CHAPTER 9

AWAKENING THE GENIUS WITHIN

"What good is it having a belly if there's no fire in it?
Wake up, drink your passion, light
a match and get to work."

–Simon Sinek

For the last 10 years, my organization has had the privilege of coaching, guiding, and advising school districts that are genuinely committed to providing the best experience for their students while helping them develop their personal, intellectual, and socioemotional skills. And I am honored to share this work with you.

Now, let's talk about you and your students and how you can put into practice what I will share in the next two chapters: a simple framework that triggers learning in students' brains. And just in case you are wondering . . . no, you do not need to be a neuroscientist for the framework to work for you. You already have what it takes: the deepest desire to enable your students to learn. You are about to discover the fastest way to enable your students to learn effectively. The six-step Relational Learning Framework consistently brings outstanding results for thousands of educators who are strategically using it to its fullest. This is a powerful way to help your students realize their potential!

Remember the 10,000-hour rule? It takes approximately 10,000 hours for someone to become an expert at anything, with proper and continuous feedback during each step of the process. Children spend roughly 16,800 hours, from kindergarten through 12th grade, sitting and waiting for someone to tell them what to do. The only feedback they get is the grade they receive at the end of each quarter, when there is nothing they can do about it. What can we expect of these students when they reach adult life? Sure, we want them to be creative and proactive, to follow their dreams, to succeed in life. Yet, we offer them no practice at this while they are at school. Instead, they become experts on doing what they are told, they get no direct and timely feedback, and many accumulate failures throughout the years!

That is why students are bored. This is the generation of now and of personalized experiences: MY friends, MY Instagram, MY message to the world with tweets, MY playlist, MY videos. It is time to personalize students' learning experience with something meaningful to them. This is the only way to engage their brains. The traditional classroom no longer serves a valuable purpose in this world of high brain stimulation. Asking students to spend one more day with a teacher in the front of the classroom and expecting them to learn anything is like going to the gym to look at people working out and hoping to lose weight without exercising.

Don't get me wrong. I know education leaders are aware of this new normal. Many are working to find solutions that engage students.

That is why we see various after-school programs, new curriculums and textbooks, and a myriad of apps being used in schools today. The challenge is that leaders expect students to put it all together without a transparent process, purpose, or meaning for themselves! All kinds of new methodologies call for "significant change," new tech, new learning environments, and so on. But the learning magic does not happen this way, because whatever these leaders are trying to foster with external resources is already within your students.

Socioeconomic differences emerge when we make learning conditional to external resources and the environment. Then, there will always be two groups: the haves and the have-nots. Equity in education comes when we start from something all students have: a brain. In our research, we found environmental factors and resources such as technology, labs, or specific textbooks can help to accelerate learning. But using those resources without a process for guiding children and educators in how to learn makes them useless.

Our research shows that, regardless of the resources available, once the brain is committed to do or learn something, it will find a way to get it done. That is how Katie and Maria, two 7th-grade students from a rural school we worked with, found a way to study music in London, even though they initially lacked the proper economic resources to do so.

By now you know that, to truly personalize your students' learning experience, you must first understand how the learning system works in the brain. Successful teachers know how learners' brains work and are equipped to take the right actions to trigger their intrinsic motivation to learn. You shouldn't have to fly blind in your efforts to teach each student to the best of your ability. You shouldn't have to guess and hope your students learn. You need to move forward knowing exactly what to do from your side, without guessing at anything.

~ THE NEUROLOGICAL FOUNDATION OF THE RELATIONAL LEARNING FRAMEWORK ~

In earlier chapters, we began to explore how learning works in the human brain. Now, I'll offer you concrete ways to tap into your students' biological intelligence. In this chapter and following, we will do a deep dive into each of the six steps of the Relational Learning Framework. You will have an easy-to-use blueprint with everything you need to get started, create a truly personalized experience for your students, and develop their learning autonomy. First, I'll show you how to enable your students to learn effectively and develop crucial socioemotional skills through a single process. Once you understand this part, we will explore strategies for each of the six steps in the Relational Learning Framework that will consistently guide learners to academic and personal success.

Relational Learning is a combination of several research-based strategies and practices proven to improve student academic achievement, social behavior, engagement in school, and community involvement.[58] Cognitive research shows that educational programs should challenge students to link, connect, and integrate ideas, taking into account their perceptions of real-world problems.[59]

Relational Learning puts the student at the center of the process as an active, rather than a passive learner,[60] with an increase in responsibility and accountability.[61] Through regular one-on-one meetings in which student and teacher reflect together on the student's progress, educators are able to personalize each student's learning pathway. Student feedback is a vital means of targeting prior knowledge and developing learning competencies.[62]

By regularly interacting one-on-one with students, educators identify suitable ways to approach student learning and tap into learning styles and multiple intelligences. Relational Learning's priority is the need for students to access and integrate different learning modes in order to increase opportunities to access and retain new knowledge.[63] Because students are also the arbiters of their learning within the Relational Learning Framework, student choice will invoke critical thinking, decision-making, reflection, and action.[64]

During the last six decades, academics have researched and concluded that one-on-one is the best educational approach.[65] The educational methodology must adapt to students and enable them to work with their own **unique learning pace**. Learning autonomy is a basic tenet of motivating students to independently seek out information, develop skill sets they can later apply throughout self-directed learning, generate an inborn capacity to take on tasks, become responsible for their own learning, and determine the direction they will take.[66]

The Relational Learning Framework supports the area of knowledge built by educational researcher Dr. David Ausubel's theory of meaningful learning[67] and well-known research on learning from experience and evaluation by Dr. Robert Marzano, Dr. Debra Pickering, and Dr. Jane Pollock.[68] Relational Learning reveals the individual's capacity to learn and grasp the world using their own skills.

~ THE PRECISE PROCESS OF DEVELOPING LEARNING AUTONOMY ~

Developing learning autonomy means developing multiple abilities through a precise skill-development process. Skill acquisition is the action of converting explicit declarative knowledge into implicit procedural knowledge. The former is the process of learning a skill, where one recites, step-by-step, what to do. The latter is the process of putting together the learned parts and making the skill an automatic action, or a habit.

Psychologists Dr. Paul Fitts and Dr. Mike Posner[69] from the University of Michigan defined three stages of skill acquisition, as follows. Although their study is related to physical human performance, we have found that it likewise applies to biological intelligence, as we will explore in detail later in this chapter.

1. **Cognitive stage:** This is the explicit, declarative knowledge stage where learning happens in the right frontal lobe through reading, thinking, processing information, and so on. Once learners understand the purpose of learning the skill, they will be motivated to practice the instructions consciously and deliberately. This stage requires attention and focus on performing each part of the task, as the deliberate practice may push a learner outside their comfort zone.

   To develop learning autonomy, the first step is to cultivate adequate goal setting and planning abilities. Students learn to be specific about their goals, set achievable and measurable metrics, and plan precise tasks to reach each goal. Then, students practice this over and over, observing how they are performing and correcting course whenever necessary, with the support of educators. The second step is to explore previous knowledge to foster the appropriate neural connections in the brain: "cells that fire together, wire together." The third step in this cognitive stage is to research the new knowledge and process what has been learned. The clear purpose of finding specific information is that it helps learners laser focus on the subject and translate new knowledge into a practical language they understand.

2. **Associative stage:** This stage is all about deliberate practice of the new knowledge. The learner may require guidance in revisiting the research to complete activities. Continuing with the example above, learners will notice significant improvement in

goal setting and planning for a few days until they reach a plateau. Educators will then assess potential areas of improvement and provide feedback to students for continuous development until they achieve mastery in each skill. In the associative stage, educators help learners "tweak" little things to improve the skill through feedback, and learners slowly eliminate mistakes.

This repetition with feedback brings excellence. After decades of observing Olympic swimmers, Dr. Daniel Chambliss, sociology professor at Hamilton College, gathered data that showed "something done consistently and correctly will produce excellence," he wrote in "The Mundanity of Excellence." It is "no more than a mundane act. The most dazzling human achievements are an aggregate of countless individual elements, each of which is, in essence, ordinary."[70] A learner must be comfortable with practicing a skill, making mistakes, and doing so repeatedly until each step is flawless by their own standards. Excellence, then, is a series of successes, practiced systematically. Discipline is having consistency to practice something every day until mastery is achieved. Discipline weighs grams, while regret weighs tons. Michael Phelps did not win 23 Olympic gold medals during his career as a swimmer just because he wanted to, but because he had the discipline to practice and improve a bit every day—thus achieving excellence.

The role of the educator is crucial at this stage. Dr. Anders Ericsson from Florida State University found in his research that immediate feedback is the most critical action to guide practice to mastery. Desire and hard work alone will not lead to improved performance. Only the right and deliberate practice with the appropriate feedback, carried through enough time, will lead to improvement and mastery. Deliberate practice means setting stretch goals, evaluating results, and finding ways to improve. As the performance of learners improves, so does their self-efficacy and confidence in the skill. This, in turn, leads to growth of their intrinsic motivation.

There are three important steps in developing learning autonomy during this stage. The first step is practice, where students internalize what they learned through exercises, games, projects, essays, videos, and so on. The second step is relating the new knowledge to their lives. Whatever they learn has a real applicability, and students themselves must be able to give it use. The third step is continuous self-assessment, in which learners reflect on their reasoning and actions, and use the conclusions to improve themselves. This self-assessment, or metacognition process, is done across all three steps, as personal feedback on the learners' progress.

3. **Autonomous stage**: In this stage, the learner can execute a skill effortlessly. The skill is already "recorded" in the brain; it is part of the learner as a habit. This is probably where you're at in driving a car or riding a bike: You do not *think* about how to drive your car or ride your bike. You do it because you *know* you can do it. In fact, thinking about it may inhibit your ability to perform the skill. When learners reach this stage in developing the skills to be autonomous, many actions become innate for them: finding meaning in what they learn, knowing what they are capable of, setting challenging and achievable goals, developing strategies to reach those goals, following a specific learning process to learn anything with a purpose, self-assessing their progress, and applying what they learn to their lives. That is what lifelong learning is all about. In this ever-changing age, the

best skill we can help students develop is the ability to transform themselves at a consistent pace with the world.

When systematically applied, the Relational Learning Framework uses the natural mechanics of the brain to make learning happen. With this framework, you help your students develop intrinsic motivation and discover what makes their contribution unique and valuable to the world. The continuous practice will bring excellence. Learners will believe in themselves so much that they will know they can accomplish anything.

The first step is for educators to support learners on a journey of continuous self-discovery so they develop intrinsic motivation. The next step is for educators to nurture autonomous learning as they guide students in developing their own potential. Education must focus on human development, rather than curriculum and content. We are making a case to shift the use of curriculum and content to enable human achievement.

Imagine that you have 100% of your students excited about learning, ready to explore the next topic, enabled to find meaning and value in what they are learning, and clearly seeing the link between what they are learning and their lives. Wouldn't it be fantastic? A teacher's dream come true? Unfortunately, this is not what is happening in the average classroom. Students are disengaged and distracted more than ever. They think 70,000-plus thoughts per day, and these are most likely not related to anything you taught them two minutes ago.

So how do you fully engage students? You are about to find out how thousands of educators are using the power from within to break through students' distractions and struggles to learn. The first step is to understand how the brain's learning system works, as we did in chapter 5. When students learn something that excites them, their brains release the right amount of dopamine and endorphins, which creates a strong bond among their brain's neurons. They have learned something valuable to them!

As you may recall from earlier chapters, when students are stressed out because of the next exam, or bored because something does not make sense to them, their brains release epinephrine, which is the "fight or flight" neurotransmitter related to stress. This leads them to disengage. This is the typical reaction when students are required to memorize and then regurgitate information. They are underutilizing their brains and finding no meaning or value in the subject. The science shows: The more excited we are about new knowledge, the stronger the neural connections. As Hebb famously observed: "Cells that fire together, wire together."

Here is an example to illustrate how easy it is to understand a new topic using previous knowledge. Let us assume you know very little about artificial intelligence. If I want to explain to you how it works, it would go something like this: AI provides you with a specific result after analyzing data through algorithms, which are procedures with a finite number of steps frequently involving repetition of an operation. It is like baking a cake: The data are your ingredients, and the algorithm is your cake recipe. Follow the recipe using the required ingredients—or in the case of AI, execute the algorithm using the data—and you will have a delicious cake. Now, the next time someone asks you to define artificial intelligence, you can explain it with the baking-a-cake metaphor. You learned this new concept rather quickly because we linked it to a neural network you already have.

The secret to activating learning is to use the right strategy to stimulate the correct neurotransmitters. Here is why this is so important: We have 70,000-plus thoughts in one day. Some 90% of these thoughts are about the past, which lead us to the same choices, behaviors, and emotions we have experienced in the past.[71] Left alone, the likelihood of these thoughts leaning toward bad habits is very high, especially when there is no proper brain stimulation. The only way to change this is to learn something new that will give us a new perspective. Then we can take action with a specific goal in mind and work until we reach that goal. When we do this, we are growing cognitive and socioemotional skills at the same time.

By the way, this also explains why student suspensions from school are useless. Punishment won't improve students' choices, behaviors, and emotions. Helping them learn something that excites them will. What we've discovered is that using the Relational Learning Framework helps generate student excitement about studying a school's required curriculum.

So, let's finish up the neuroscience of learning. The brain is the most powerful tool in the universe. It "talks" to us all the time, driving our actions without us even thinking, often by using habits. This is the reason you can ride a bike even if you haven't done so for many years. As educators, our objective is to help learners foster cognitive and socioemotional development, and use their brains wisely by creating outstanding habits.

Now you understand your students already have what it takes: a brain.

~ A REMINDER: THE IMPORTANCE OF HABITS ~

In what's been called the Knowledge Era, the effective use of our brains is the 21st-century's gold mine. The brain really loves habits and it is unable to differentiate between good and bad ones. That's because a habit uses less mental energy by reducing the amount of decision-making required from moment to moment. Habits are a preservation tool that has served us well for millennia. For learners, good habits are a key ally in success, while bad habits prevent them from achieving their full potential. To produce effective learning results, we must create outstanding learning habits.

~ GETTING STARTED WITH THE RELATIONAL LEARNING FRAMEWORK ~

Now you are ready to learn about the six-step Relational Learning Framework and how it enables your students to learn effectively as soon as tomorrow. Simply build your learning units using the framework and witness brains at work! This is a framework teachers can use to break down the learning process. Students will realize they can learn anything using this framework, and will begin to recognize opportunities to master a new skill and form good habits. Outstanding outcomes become a predictable consequence once students start using the six-step Relational Learning Framework.

These are the six steps of the Relational Learning Framework:

1. Goal Setting and Planning
2. Explore
3. Research
4. Practice
5. Relate
6. Self-Assess

Now, let's explore each step in depth.

STEP 1: GOAL SETTING AND PLANNING

Have you noticed that whenever you want to do something big, you come up with a specific plan? The very first steps to activating learning are adequate goal setting and planning. Students learn to be specific when setting their goals, to pick achievable and measurable metrics, and to plan precise tasks to reach each goal. Then, they practice repeatedly while self-observing how they perform, and correct their course whenever necessary, all with the support of educators.

This is important, because specific daily planning develops goal-setting abilities, organization, work effectiveness, decision-making through prioritization, responsibility, and accountability. Planning improves self-regulation of performance and self-monitoring of specific actions required to achieve specific goals. All these skills translate into perseverance and, consequently, personal agency.

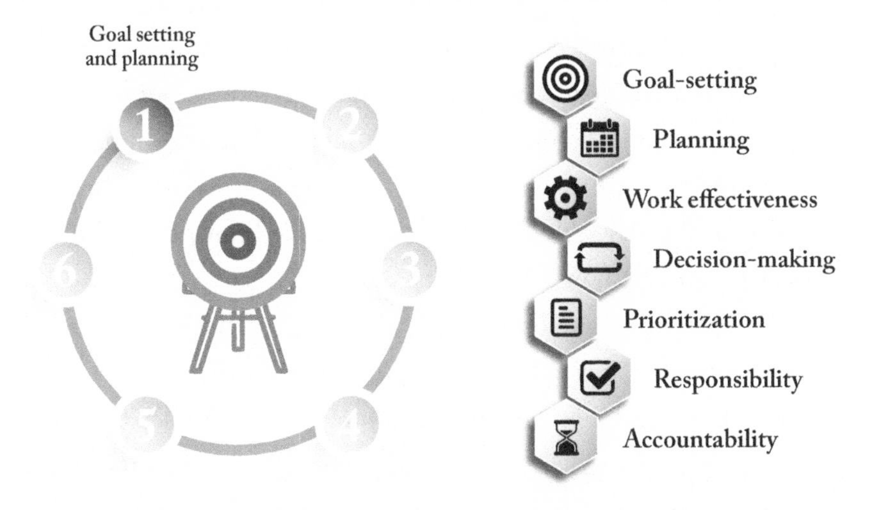

Figure 9.1: Goal Setting and Planning Step and skills developed

When we have learners set goals and plan, it forces them to state an intention. Research has found that stating clear intentions and achievable goals increases the chance of achievement by two to three times.[72]

For example, let's say you want to become a runner. If you state, "I want to become a runner" without a specific plan, it may take a while to make that happen, IF it happens. But your chances of reaching your running goal will be two to three times higher if you instead say, "I will start by walking briskly for 30 minutes every day at 6 a.m. for one week. The following week, at 6 a.m. every day I will alternate running for one minute and walking for five minutes. In the following weeks, I will continue increasing my running minutes until I can run for 30 minutes. Then I will set new goals and create a new plan."

The doing-with-a-plan part is where the magic happens. The more hours you practice something, the better you will be at executing it. Consistency is starting something and finishing it. Reasonable, bite-size goals will help you persevere. Every action you take will reinforce your vision of the person you want to become. Therefore, although goal setting and planning seem so simple, they have a profound impact on students' lives. The goal is no longer to run a marathon, but to become a runner. The goal is no longer to learn a subject, but to use knowledge with meaning and purpose aligned to a student's objectives in life. This brings a substantial release of dopamine in the brain, created by the expectation of a desirable result.

The process is the same with younger children who are unable to read and write just yet. Instead of writing their daily goals, they will draw them. Younger children are natural artists! Learners understand what they are capable of and will pursue whatever goals they set for themselves. Imagine if you and I had had the chance to learn this process while at school. We might follow that diet to the end and exercise more often, never giving lame excuses such as "work has been too demanding" or "I don't have time for it." Is that familiar to you?

As learners grow in autonomy, they start planning their week, month, year, and eventually their lives. Remember Jonathan's plan to complete one full grade in eight months? Or Katie's and Maria's decision to study music in London? It is the realization of this first step. Planning and goal setting develop intrinsic motivation as learners discover how hard they can push themselves and how far they can go. It is like sailing: Although the wind is blowing in one direction, the sailor can go anywhere because she knows how to position the sail. Regardless of the circumstances, by understanding the process, and doing the proper planning, the sailor will reach her destiny.

Students learn to visualize future rewards in the present moment, as those rewards are aligned to their personal goals. Students enjoy the learning experience when they find meaning and purpose in the tasks ahead because they understand they are capable of doing what they set out to do. To get started with this step, simply share with students the activities they will work on during that day and allow them to decide how to tackle them as a group. Then, after a week or two of practice, move to having each student set their own personal goal, independent from other students.

In the Relational Learning Framework, your students are the ones planning, not you. The more you "delegate" these tasks and allow learners to make their own decisions, the more they will be committed and motivated, and the more you are preparing them for life. Your job becomes guiding them to reach the objectives they set for themselves. With continuous practice for over 10,000 hours, you will see how valuable this first step is for you and your students.

STEP 2: EXPLORE

This step is so simple and yet so powerful, and is one of the most significant differences between the average teacher and the effective teacher. In this step, ask your students to reflect on the theme and share their preexisting knowledge. Personal experiences, everyday life, expectations, questions, doubts, and curiosity become the starting point for this exploration.

Encouraging students to explore helps them connect previous knowledge to new knowledge and accelerates learning considerably. As Hebb said, "Cells that fire together, wire together." This second step develops learners' capacity to find meaning, identify purpose, develop self-awareness, and explore past knowledge.

Thirteen-year-old Marco never had a knack for biology, but one day, he was excited to explain to me how the digestive system works by comparing it to a car, something he had a true passion for: Food is gas, the engine is the digestive system, and so on. He loves cars and explores all their features whenever he can. It is undeniable he understood the subject completely by linking the new knowledge to what he knows about cars!

This is what makes Relational Learning so different: As an educator, you ask the learner to start from their current practice and knowledge, instead of from somewhere entirely new that requires them to form completely new neural connections. Your students are like seeds—whatever they have inside of them is what will grow. You can only expect an apple seed to give you apples and an orange seed to give you oranges. If you try to grow apples from an orange seed, you will fail.

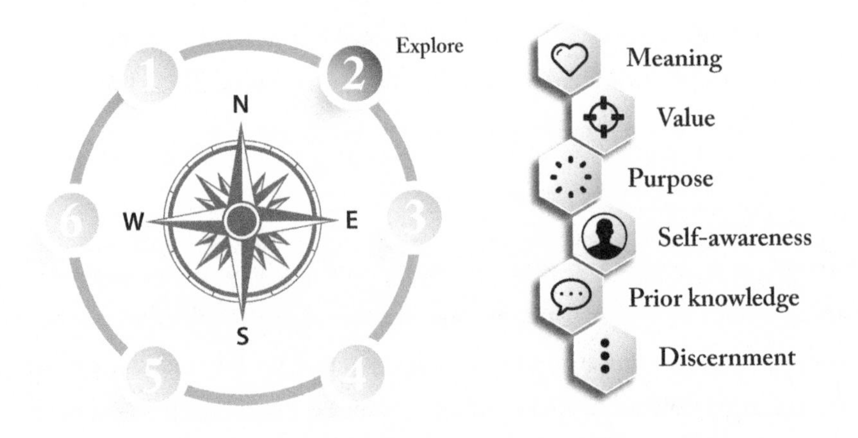

Figure 9.2: Explore Step and skills developed

How do you start from an existing seed? Students may respond to a contextualized question or hypothesize about what they will learn and achieve in the unit. For example, let's say that you are teaching music history. Typical exploratory questions would include: What is your favorite music genre? Who started it? Why? Can you associate a singer or band to each existing style? At first, you may get the typical answer: "I don't know." But with practice, students will realize they know a lot and need to connect the dots! Curiosity will flourish from then on, as learners align their personal experiences to what is being learned.

STEP 3: RESEARCH

Fourteen-year-old Anna never liked reading. She was more into music, rap to be precise. Whenever it was time to read, she would roll her eyes and put her head down on her desk, in total despair. When Anna's teachers told her she could use rap to research school subjects, she did not know how, but loved the idea. Her teacher helped her explore how this might work. Little by little, Anna found, in the music she loved, the answer to learning. She even started composing her own rap to summarize what she learned.

In this step, your students research new information about the unit of study through a wide variety of resources. These can include printed books and reports, audio books, videos, interviews, even rap music! Researching new information leads to the development of a personal knowledge base that can then be reflected in an organizational grid or a concept map that students create. See chapter 11.

Student research is so basic, and at the same time, so powerful. When teachers simply provide all the answers, it conditions students to always expect someone else to know things and to want an immediate solution for all their problems. If conditioned in that way throughout their school years, they will become experts at waiting for answers from someone else, such as an employer, a family member, or the government. These expectations can make them give up quickly when finding the answer requires too much work, and can lead to adult temper tantrums and the conclusion that life is unfair.

As learners develop research skills, they also become comfortable with the inquiry process, and develop critical thinking, reading, comprehension, and discernment. Blessed be the continuous 10,000-hour practice! Most of all, while doing their own research, learners discover that knowledge is out there for them to explore. Tens of thousands of students we worked with reported that this is the step they enjoy the most because it puts their brains to work.

To get started in this step, you need to provide resources students will use to learn more about the specific unit. Give them whatever you have available, such as textbooks, articles, a webpage, a video, a magazine, and so on. Then, provide a framework they can use to synthesize the information they find. Later, you will learn to personalize your students' learning experience with specific strategies and to enable them to find their own resources.

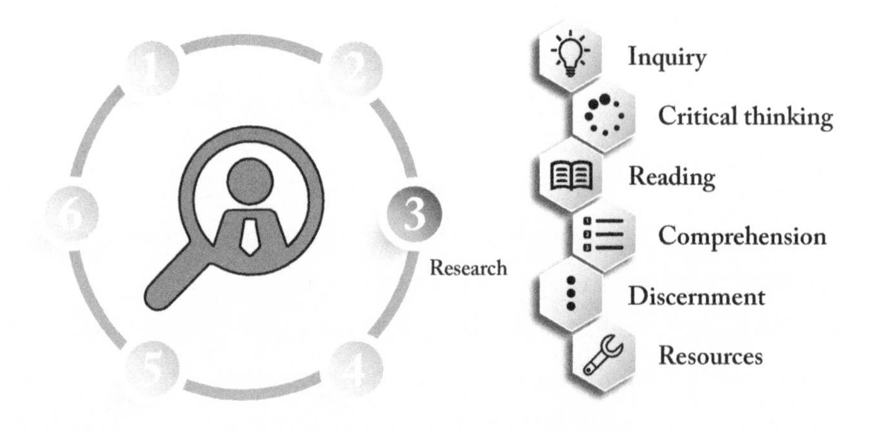

Figure 9.3: Research Step and skills developed

We have covered a lot so far. You certainly don't need to start with everything. You can just take one baby step at a time and begin introducing these practices, so you feel confident you are making all the right moves.

~ COGNITIVE AND SOCIOEMOTIONAL LEARNING IN SYMBIOSIS ~

Have you noticed how students learn content while developing critical cognitive and socioemotional skills? They are intrinsically related, and learners will practice them with the Relational Learning Framework.

Here's a quick rundown:

Step 1: Goal Setting and Planning helps students develop:

- goal-setting abilities, when they set goals daily and precisely, with clear metrics;
- planning skills, as they are able to distribute tasks throughout the day;
- organization, as they identify the resources necessary to execute a plan;
- work effectiveness, as they get the job done;
- decision-making through prioritization, as they have access to the big picture of everything that needs to be done, and therefore prioritize and decide when to do what;
- responsibility, as they are now in charge of accomplishing what they committed to;

- accountability, as they know they can deliver the planned activities within a certain timeframe;
- self-regulation, because they are committed to deliverables in a period of time;
- self-monitoring skills, as they are aware of the task they must accomplish, along with the timeframe they set for themselves;
- self-esteem, as they understand they are capable of accomplishing what they set out to do; and
- personal agency, as they take ownership of their learning process.

Step 2: Explore develops each learner's capacity to:

- find meaning and value in what they are learning, as they connect previous knowledge to the new knowledge;
- identify the purpose of knowledge, as they add new knowledge to what they already know;
- develop self-awareness, as they explore previous knowledge; and
- explore past knowledge and discover they know more than they think.

Step 3: Research helps learners develop:

- inquiry skills, when they learn to ask questions in order to acquire the appropriate resources;

- critical thinking, as they are constantly evaluating whether new information they find makes sense;
- reading and comprehension, as they have to read and register their conclusions in an organizational grid or a concept map;
- discernment, as they learn to evaluate whether various research resources are trustworthy; and
- the capacity to identify useful resources, as they will eventually find their own resources in addition to the resources provided by teachers.

Peter was diagnosed with learning disabilities from the day he was born. His mother had an issue during delivery, which deprived the baby of oxygen in his brain for a couple of minutes. The boy was growing up highly dependent on his mother and sister to dress, eat, go to school, do his homework, and so on. Peter attends a "normal" school, as there were no other schools offering special education programs in the area. We started working with his school when Peter was in 6th grade. He was late in his cognitive development and could only complete about 20% of the year's curriculum. His engagement was minimal to none.

As they learned and used the Relational Learning Framework, Peter's teachers slowly shifted their focus from curriculum to learning process. Peter started learning to plan, to explore his previous knowledge, to research, and to understand what he was reading. It took about two years of practice for Peter to use these steps to create a learning process habit, whereas his classmates were able to do so in about three months. Peter's teachers respected his unique learning pace, though. Today, Peter learns autonomously, with minimal intervention by his teachers. He is more social, as he is now aware of his capacities and no longer compares himself to others. His mother is overwhelmed with happiness, as her child arrives home with all of his schoolwork done. He even helps with home chores and no longer needs his mother and sister to help him dress, eat, or anything else. Peter is clearly capable of succeeding in his life, regardless of how someone labeled him in the past. "I am now independent," said Peter about himself, at the age of 16.

~ TRAPS TO AVOID ~

Now, as I mentioned earlier, my organization works with thousands of teachers every year. We've had the opportunity to witness firsthand some outstanding success stories of average teachers who have gone from struggling to help even one student succeed to making significant progress with all of their students. And we've seen what holds other teachers back from ever helping their learners achieve the level of success they want. I want to make you aware of these traps so you can avoid getting stuck.

1. Conclude that your students are unable to complete these steps because you see no results in the short-term.

   The first few times your students plan and set goals, explore their previous knowledge, and do their own research, they may require significant support from you. Avoid concluding that they are incapable of completing these steps, either because they are too young or because you see no effort on their part. Remind yourself that this is something new for them and, with practice, the process will become natural. The younger they are when they learn these steps, the better. If they do not know how to read and write yet, they can plan, explore their knowledge, and research via drawings. Remember when you learned to ride a bike? This is the same concept! Do you *know* you can ride a bike or *think* you can?

Allow your students to practice these skills every day and you will see results in time. Keep in mind that students are different, and some will learn faster than others, but all of them can do it. Trust me, that's what my team and I experience in our work with thousands of teachers.

2. Believe you can only give students personal attention when you're working with a small group.

   You may believe you can only work with a small number of students if you want to be able to give attention to each of them. This is true if you insist on using the same traditional practices of teaching to the class. With the Relational Learning Framework, you can start working with the students as a group until they understand how each step works, and then you will see them taking the initiative to follow the steps by themselves. They will develop the habit of following these steps to learn anything. Your role will begin to move from teaching to coaching, and you'll be able to give each student personal attention. Students will be in different learning stages throughout a given day. Some of them will require your guidance and some will be working by themselves. It means each day you have to provide guidance to some of your students, but you don't have to provide guidance to all of them every day.

3. Decide that your class periods are too short to use the Relational Learning Framework.

   Your class is 50 minutes long and you must deliver specific content in that time frame. It may feel like you don't have enough time to get through all your content, let alone allow students to make their way through the Relational Learning Framework. But you can accomplish all you and your students need to in the allotted time. It just takes practice.

Remember the first time you cooked a meal? It was overwhelming to measure the amount of each ingredient and make sure nothing was burning, while triple-checking the recipe. But, after practicing for a while, you can probably cook without even thinking about it.

Your students will experience the same thing. After they practice planning, exploring previous knowledge, and researching over and over, eventually they will not even need to consult with you. You will experience your students' agency developing right in front of you. You and your students will do more in 50 minutes than you ever imagined. Just to give you an idea, 37% of students engaged in Relational Learning finish one full grade in seven months. Educators find that they need to increase content and activities because students learn so fast!

4. Students having difficulties in a subject are unable to make decisions about their learning.

   When students are having a difficult time in a subject, you may be tempted to step in and take over their learning process, rather than allowing them to continue following the Relational Learning Framework. Don't. Letting them continue to work through difficulties may be outside your comfort zone, but let me reaffirm that you can do it. We've seen it happen with so many teachers!

   As for your students having difficulty in your subject, we have found that, because of learning gaps throughout the years,

> students are uninterested in exploring something they haven't grasped entirely or have been told they are not good at it. Remember: No one is born not liking math or social studies, or anything else! They learn not to like it because they do not see that is has value and meaning for their lives. If you help them find meaning and value in what they learn, they will enjoy the experience. This is what the Relational Learning Framework is designed to do. Each step will get your students closer to seeing value in what they are learning. Your frustrations will be long-gone when learners become fully engaged with your subject.

Richard, a science teacher, reflected how common it is to disregard students' passion. Before using the Relational Learning Framework, he believed teaching was all about providing reading materials and ensuring students transcribe the information on their notebooks. Now he understands that, when students use their talents to demonstrate learning, they truly possess the concepts of any subject.

In one unit of study, Richard's students Laura and Julian learned about how to be responsible with the environment while exploring agriculture. Laura and Julian came up with a comic to explain the concepts they learned. Laura is really good at storytelling and Julian expresses his creativity through drawing and colors. Both of them understood the concept, for sure!

When students go through each learning step themselves, motivation to learn becomes intrinsic and personal. It is a process that stimulates the correct neurotransmitters and, therefore, increases the chances of strongly bonded neural connections.

To Richard's surprise, the creative process continued way after the unit of study was done. Laura and Julian invited other kids from school, created their own costumes with recyclable material, and acted out the comic, all recorded for posterity. With his eyes watering, Richard said, "I can only imagine how much fun they had, the laughs in each practice. . . . It reminds me of my own childhood. My students used their talents as an excuse to demonstrate learning. I hope other students can do the same."

CHAPTER 10

FEEDING THE GENIUS WITHIN

"If you are going to doubt something,
doubt your own limits."

–Don Ward

Remember Brian, the student diagnosed with ADHD and dyslexia? What would have become of Brian's life if his teachers were unable to tap into his potential? Brian was lucky to attend a school that used the Relational Learning Framework. Yet, so many people in the world are living and dying with their potential completely unrealized. Brian understands now that the power of his success is in his hands. He no longer believes he has limitations with learning.

The genius of your students is waiting to be ignited. It starts with *your* belief that learners have what it takes: a brain. With that brain, they can reach 100% of their potential. And learning is what everyone needs to continually make good choices, exhibit good behaviors, and experience healthy emotions.

The next steps in the Relational Learning Framework consolidate cognitive and socioemotional learning while students internalize a specific subject. Ready?

~ CONTINUING WITH THE RELATIONAL LEARNING FRAMEWORK ~

STEP 4: PRACTICE

This is the process of internalizing what has been learned. In this step, you activate the student's capacity to transform or improve the prior knowledge identified in the second step. This stage includes activities planned by you or suggested by learners, as they gain learning autonomy. Examples of activities are exercises, games, group projects, essays, video producing, and songwriting.

Traditional educational models jump almost directly to this step, after briefly exposing students to the subject's theory through a lecture. When that happens, the possibility of the learner's brain releasing dopamine and serotonin to make learning stick is close to zero. This is because students are unable to identify the meaning and value of the content for them. They haven't connected this new knowledge to their previous knowledge.

When students execute the steps of the Relational Learning Framework themselves, they develop intrinsic and personal motivation to learn. That process stimulates the right neurotransmitters and, therefore, increases the chances of strongly bonded neural connections.

The practice step fosters creativity, collaboration, leadership, and project-based learning through activities that you and your students agree upon. As learners gain more autonomy to move through Steps 1–4, their brains get used to the sweet spot of neurotransmitter levels that enable them to learn effectively.

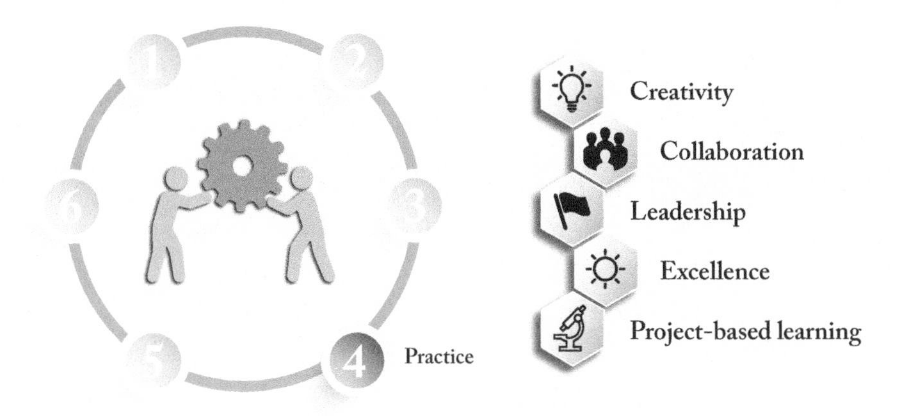

Figure 10.1: Practice Step and skills developed

STEP 5: RELATE

In this step, students realize the real purpose and meaning of the unit by relating what they have learned to their own lives, through specific activities and reflection. It is so simple, yet so important! You can tell learners thousands of times why you think it's important that they learn something, and they may remember the information for a test. But unless learners identify the use of this knowledge by themselves, they will simply not learn. The neural connections will just be too weak.

It is like trying to describe how to run a marathon. You may be able to do it because you read a book or watched a video about it. However, unless you have a personal practical use for it, you will eventually forget it. When we enable students to organize knowledge into practical application in their lives, it becomes useful knowledge and brings them personal value. Knowledge is only "potential power." It becomes "power" to learners when it has a purpose with a definite end for its applicability.

Figure 10.2: Relate Step and skills developed

Students learn to relate the new knowledge to their lives and discover its practical applicability by answering this question: How will I use what I learned? Their answer will help them find connections to what's already in their brains and at the core of their soul. We saw that in the way Marco compared the digestive system to cars, and Laura and Julian used their talents to share how to protect the environment.

STEP 6: SELF-ASSESS

Metacognition is the ability to self-assess one's own reasoning and actions, using the outcome to improve oneself. With practice, metacognition becomes a powerful tool of self-awareness and self-improvement, allowing an individual to find meaning in life. Continuous self-improvement creates inner peace, and therefore, a better quality of life. Children CAN learn to self-assess while in a safe school environment. By allowing learners to choose a path and experience the consequences of their choices, we help them become aware of how decisions impact their reality.

This practice will prepare learners to avoid a lifetime of regrets, as they practice self-awareness from an early age to design their future.

There is a more robust way to self-assess, which you can learn in our professional development series. But for now, you can get off to a solid start by asking a few questions of your learners once they have done steps one to five of the Relational Learning Framework.

Questions to Help Learners Self-Assess:

- How do you feel?
- How long did it take to finish your unit?
- Were your goals clear?
- Have you used more or less time than you allotted to this task?

Students may get tangled up when they try to answer these questions at first, as they are used to criticism and strive to avoid making mistakes. Encourage them to share their self-evaluation and what they will do differently next time.

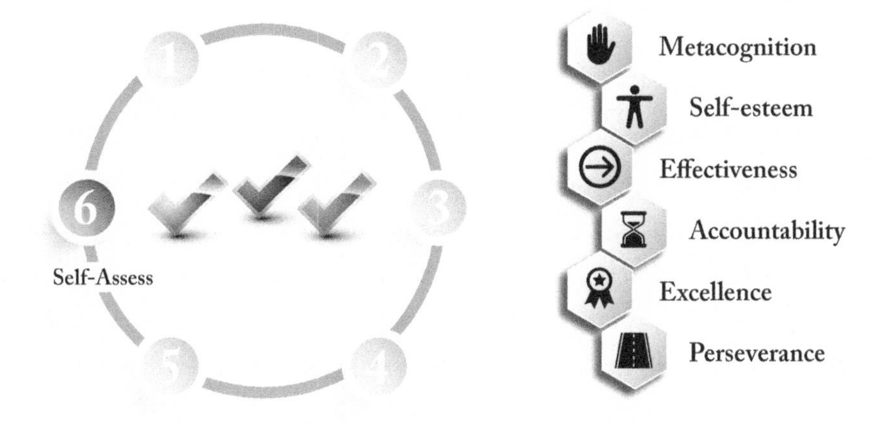

Figure 10.3: Self-Assess Step and skills developed

You can start by asking learners to self-assess after they finish each step. Ask questions to explore how they found a certain piece of information, their thinking process, and their plans to proceed to the next learning step. As this process becomes a habit and they gain learning autonomy, allow them to go through two to three steps at a time before self-assessing their progress.

~ KEYS TO MAKING THE RELATIONAL LEARNING FRAMEWORK WORK ~

Allow students to complete each learning step as their capacity permits at this time. Now, this is very important: *Do not expect perfection* and *do not compare one student's work to another's.* Learners are getting used to this practice, and each of them will get there in a different time frame. Their prefrontal cortex is in full throttle! It is the same experience you might have trying to learn a new language: Your head will hurt at first, but, eventually, speaking the new language becomes natural to you.

Don't throw everything at your learners at once. Give them one thing to focus on in the next unit of study, such as improving their answers on the organizational grid (see chapter 11) or finding a different resource to research.

Praise the progress in the learning process! You help learners self-assess each step of the way because they need small wins to start feeding their "I-can-do-this" attitude. The more evidence students have that they can do it, the more they will believe in it.[73] You are helping them build intrinsic motivation and perseverance through metacognition. No external exam, person, or tech will develop grit—only students themselves can do so.

How about required exams or standardized tests? When educators apply Relational Learning systematically, their students are better prepared for tests. They remember the content more easily because it is associated with areas of their lives. If they do not recall certain content, it is easy to go back to their notes and review organizational grids or concept maps, which summarize what was learned. Granted, grades are less important than the learning process in Relational Learning, but since the education system values academic grading in order to open doors for college and careers, students must go through exams.

As one public school principal described it: "Relational Learning is the answer for high-quality public education because it prepares students for life. The market today prioritizes competencies over the content. Students learn and practice competencies while studying the required content."

By now, we are connecting the dots of the six-step Relational Learning Framework. It is so simple, yet so powerful.

- REVIEW: THE SIX-STEP RELATIONAL LEARNING FRAMEWORK -

Step 1: Goal setting and planning, when students develop self-awareness of what they are capable of, and the capacity to push their limits.

Step 2: Explore, when students realize they already have a starting point to learn from, even if it is something unrelated to the subject.

Step 3: Research, when students use a variety of resources to learn more about a subject and come to understand that knowledge is out there for them to explore.

Step 4: Practice, which fosters creativity, collaboration, leadership, and project-based learning. The step strengthens neural connections.

Step 5: Relate, when students develop the ability to communicate, speak publicly, find relevance, and practice real-world problem solving.

Step 6: Self-assess, which fosters metacognition and self-esteem, and develops effectiveness, accountability, excellence, and perseverance.

As you can see, the Relational Learning Framework is the practical application of personalized learning, project-based learning, competency-based learning, and autonomous learning—simplified in only six steps. Throughout this learning process, which is aligned with how the brain works, students are developing 21st-century skills and competencies for life. So why insist on working any other way? No more guessing how students learn, no more "teaching to the middle," no more leaving any potential behind. You can start applying the Relational Learning Framework as soon as today! Check out some examples of units of study using the six steps and download your free unit of study template to build your units on our website: BecomingEinsteinsTeacher.com.

Remember the meaning of the word education comes from Latin *educare*, which means "to bring forth from within." Therefore, if we truly want students to learn, we must start from within! That is why the Relational Learning Framework works so well. It fosters student agency when students take the lead in their learning and when they develop critical skills to take the lead in their lives.

By now, you know you are perfectly capable of using the Relational Learning Framework. The more you practice it, the more you will have the confidence to make your students successful. This framework is the result of decades of pedagogical research and development, carefully crafted to be easy to use in any context: rural or urban schools, any textbook, with or without technology, small or large classrooms, and with learners of various levels. Your students already have what it takes: a brain. Your job is to ignite the best of it to benefit those students for life.

Imagine your classroom as a dynamic environment where learning is happening effortlessly. That's the goal of Relational Learning. Remember the quote: "Give a man a fish, and you feed him for a day. Teach a man to fish, and you feed him for a lifetime"? You are doing precisely that, teaching students to learn through strategic skills they can use to learn anything they want in life.

Figure 10.4: In the Relational Learning Framework, students learn to learn while developing competencies

CHAPTER 11

TOOLS FOR LIFE

"It's your road and yours alone. Others may walk it with you, but no one can walk it for you."

–RUMI

Relational Learning utilizes research to test and challenge existing models of theory and practice, always aiming at the framework's scalability to ensure it can be easily adopted for large education systems around the world. One existing model through which we have examined Relational Learning is the teaching and learning research of Dr. Benjamin Bloom from the University of Chicago and Northwestern University. In 1984, Bloom published an article in the academic journal *Education Researcher* titled *The 2 Sigma Problem: The Search for Methods of Group Instruction as Effective as One-to-One Tutoring.*

In the article, Bloom established 19 variables for effectively improving student academic achievement and evaluated how much each variable influences learning outcomes. At the bottom of the list, he found that resources such as textbooks and technology, along with students' socioeconomic backgrounds, made the smallest contribution to achieving high levels of learning. Bloom then tested those variables in three instruction conditions:

1. The conventional classroom
2. Mastery instruction, which adds feedback and corrective procedures to a conventional classroom
3. One-to-one tutoring

Bloom found that one-to-one tutoring improved student achievement the most, with results two standard deviations (two sigma) above the conventional classroom. The same result was consistent in many other observations.

On one hand, it was great news: Regardless of their background, previous level of academic achievement, or access to specific resources, each student would achieve the same outstanding results with one-to-one tutoring. On the other hand, this one-teacher-per-student solution has an unbearable cost for the education system, which makes it impossible to scale. The two-sigma problem was born: How can educators attain these high levels of achievement seen in one-to-one tutoring in a group setting? In other words, how can one teacher provide a personalized experience to multiple students at once, and still achieve these results?

Bloom found that students can attain high academic achievement if they develop good learning habits, improve reading skills, and devote time to learning. He also found that emphasizing higher mental processes enables students to relate their learning to the contexts in which they live. “These abilities are regarded as one step of essential characteristics needed to continue learning and to cope with a rapidly changing world,” he concluded.

Bloom and his colleagues were looking at a simple, scalable method that could be used by any teacher to achieve results similar to one-to-one tutoring. Educators could learn this method quickly and implement it inexpensively. Such a method, he wrote, “would be an educational contribution of the greatest magnitude. It would change popular notions about human potential and would have significant effects on what the schools can and should do with the education years each society requires of its young people.”

The six-step Relational Learning Framework is a practical solution for Bloom’s two-sigma problem, as it is an intuitive, low-cost method that teachers can easily incorporate into their practice in order to develop human potential through learning. It incorporates a personal learning experience in which students make practical use of their new knowledge and develop agency in their own learning and lives.

You are now familiar with the six-step Relational Learning Framework and how each step develops cognitive and social-emotional skills. Let’s examine two tools to bring your implementation of the framework alive:

1. Goal setting and planning
2. Units of study

~ GOAL SETTING AND PLANNING ~

Traditionally, we believe the responsible students are the ones who sit all day without talking much, do everything teachers say, and do well on tests. However, if responsibility comes once you plan and take action, when did these students ever plan or act? They are *obedient* students with no practice in transforming themselves. They sit down, wait for the next instruction, and execute to the teacher's preferences. What can we expect from these students as they reach adulthood?

Responsibility is a conscious decision to do something that you know will have an outcome, and a decision to face the consequences of your action, whether they are good or bad. As global best-selling author Jack Canfield writes in his book *The Success Principles*, "One of the most important principles for success is taking 100% responsibility for your life and your results." We can offer students practice taking 100% responsibility for their 16,800 hours in school and the consequence of doing so are that they will become successful in life.

Thus, the very first step in the Relational Learning Framework is to incorporate the fundamental skill students will need to start each day: goal setting and planning. Specific daily planning develops goal-setting abilities, organization, work effectiveness, decision-making through prioritizing, responsibility, and accountability. Planning improves self-regulation of performance and self-monitoring of specific actions required to achieve specific goals. Small wins at setting and achieving specific daily goals increase a learner's confidence and motivation to continue setting and achieving goals.

As learners get used to the process of goal setting and planning daily, they become aware of their personal limitations, what they are capable of, and what they have to do to reach their goals. They are then able to expand their goal setting across longer time periods and multiple goals—an important component of developing perseverance and learning autonomy. They also develop intrinsic motivation as they discover how hard they can push themselves and how far they can go. Learners start planning their week, month, and year.

You will notice, over time, that learners will even start planning their lives. They will set their minds on what they want to do, who they want to be, where they want to go. This is what happened with George, who I met when he was 12 years old. He told me he would study mechatronics in Germany, at a specific university he chose because, he explained, "there are two top universities for this career in the world, one in the U.S. and one in Germany. I picked the one in Germany." He knew how to get a scholarship and was already working on doing so. No one had to tell him what to do. He did it by himself! This is how daily goal setting, planning, and self-assessment practices will enable learners to plan their lives. We just need to help them discover their innate ability to have new ideas and act upon them.

- START THE DAY COACHING STUDENTS IN GOAL SETTING AND PLANNING -

To get started, the very first activity at the beginning of each day is to coach learners to set goals, plan, and make decisions about priorities. They should also have measurable metrics that are within their capacity. These goals should be based on students' current unit of study, which means your students must have access to the activities they will work on during that day. Students will be making decisions about their learning plan or work, including which activities to do first and how to prioritize those activities.

You can start by having students make group goals together. As your students develop this skill, move to having each of them set personal goals. While older children will write their goals down, younger children who are unable to read and write just yet should instead draw their daily goals.

Start with small, simple goals, such as reading the activities of the first learning stage and completing the first activity. With that, you are coaching learners to develop self-control, which requires a lot of energy from the prefrontal cortex before it becomes a habit. At this point, it is essential that you continuously praise each learner's *effort* in the process, not how intelligent or smart they are. Your praise is the reward needed for the learner's brain to produce dopamine naturally while they are practicing this skill. As you notice learners mastering their practice, challenge them to increase the number of activities they plan and have them set a goal to complete all activities that day. Small successes motivate learners to continue investing in skill development, one manageable step at a time.

~ END THE DAY COACHING STUDENTS IN SELF-EVALUATION OF THEIR PLANNING ~

At the end of the day, coach learners to self-evaluate the results of their goal setting and planning, and help them reflect on their capacity to accomplish what they planned. If learners are achieving 100% of their daily goals, challenge them to increase the number of daily activities they set for themselves. If not, help them reflect on how to plan within their capacity. In this process, learners discover their limits, enabling them to develop self-awareness and increase their self-esteem.

Stanford psychologist Dr. Albert Bandura, whose work we touched on in earlier chapters, conducted extensive research into overcoming doubts about one's own capacity. He concluded that by guiding an individual through small successes they can be led to alter their belief that they don't have the capacity to accomplish something.[74] These small successes, often achieved with guidance, can positively impact the rest of a person's life, preparing them for persevering through tougher challenges.

~ ADD IN WEEKLY AND MONTHLY PLANNING ~

As soon as learners incorporate daily planning into their practice, add weekly planning at the beginning of each week. It will expand learners' vision of the near future. Then, as soon as learners are comfortable with weekly and daily planning, incorporate monthly planning at the start of each new month. Moving from daily to monthly planning takes about six weeks or less.

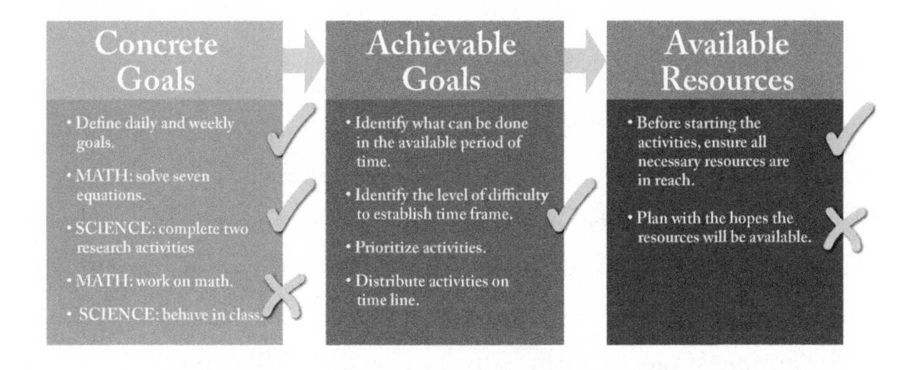

Figure 11.1: Examples of concrete, achievable goals

It is crucial that you move learners from daily planning to monthly and eventually yearly planning as soon as possible. They must learn to have an ultimate goal in life in order to develop intrinsic motivation to do today's tasks.

It will surely take a bit longer than six weeks for your youngest students to internalize planning as a daily activity, so make sure this is the very first activity of the day, every day. Make it a routine, and eventually, it will become a habit, even for the littlest ones. Younger children exposed to this decision-making process early in their lives will greatly benefit from it later.

Remember, intrinsic motivation is related to passion. The more we discover and expose each learner's passion, the more intrinsically motivated they will be. Students learn effectively because they want to, not because you told them to, and you want to hold on to or recapture that. Coach learners to look at their bright future ahead. To fully realize their passion, they will need a plan and they will practice to realize their passion while acquiring the skills they need. Learners will develop intrinsic motivation by working on something that interests them. They will spend hours on it, well aware of their cognitive control over what they are doing.

~ ALWAYS SET CONCRETE, ACHIEVABLE, MEASURABLE GOALS ~

You want your students to accomplish the goals they set. This means the goals need to be concrete and achievable, and that you need the resources on hand for students to accomplish those goals.

Imagine you are helping a 5th-grade student improve his reading. He has been in remedial classes and his parents are worried he will fall further behind. You know this student loves to dance. A goal setting and planning strategy for this student would look like this:

1. **Find the related resources**: Gather books, articles, magazines, etc. related to dancing.

2. **Set small goals**: I will read one page per day.

3. **Conduct daily planning**: Today, I will read one page and fill up the organizational grid related to this page. I will write one paragraph to explain what I understood.

4. **Evaluate daily goals at the end of each day**: Was I able to achieve my daily goal? Do I need to improve? What will I do better tomorrow?

5. **Celebrate daily wins:** Reevaluate my goal if I were unable to accomplish it. In this self-evaluation process, never ask, "*Why* can't I do this?" Instead, say, "My strategy did not work. *How* can I do this better?"

6. **Increase goals little by little:** I read one page faster than usual. Now I will challenge myself and read one additional page every day.

7. **Weekly measurement:** How many pages did I read? How much did I understand about what I read? Celebrate weekly accomplishments!

Fill out this section at "Plan and set goals" step

Fill out this section at the "Metacognition" step

BEFORE I START WORKING ON THE UNIT		WHEN I AM DONE WITH THE UNIT		
STEP	MY GOAL Think: "I will do *this* to achieve *that*, in *X* amount of time"	DID I MAKE IT? YES	NO	IMPROVEMENT OPPORTUNITIES Think: "To improve my goals, I can . . ."
Goal Setting and Planning	Read the activities and write my goals on this template, to set my expectations. –30 minutes	☒	☐	Stuck to my planning this time!
Explore	Complete the prompts, to get into the topic. – 30 minutes	☒	☐	Plenty of time to do this activity.
Research	Watch videos and analyze them to synthetize information. –1.50 hours	☒	☐	Keep watching videos and read the daily Relational Education tips that I get in my email.
Practice	Write an essay to organize my ideas. – 1 hour	☒	☐	Share this essay with my colleagues.
Relate	Write a letter to remind myself to keep progressions. –1 hour	☒	☐	Keep my letter!
Self-assess	Self-assess if I reached the goals I am writing on this template, to keep improving my planning skills. –30 minutes	☒	☐	Keep improving my time management skills.

Formulate goals: Verb (Infinitive) + What + For what

Reflect and propose strategies you can implement at the next opportunity.

Figure 11.2: Example of daily and weekly planning

Award-winning author John Irving said the following about the process of writing: "The moment when a book is published, the window when it is available to the public and people are talking to you about it, is very small. It is over in a couple of months! But the book might have taken four, five, six, seven years [to be written]. And the next book will take a comparable amount of time. I learned from wrestling that you better love the process itself, you better love the practicing, repeating the same move 100 times with the same boring sporting partner. An inch at a time, then crossing something out, moving this sentence here, taking that sentence and putting it there. It is slow! People would fall asleep watching a writer write or a wrestler in practice." Irving learned to love the process. It is what we must aim for—to have learners love the learning process by practicing it over, and over, and over again.

As students see their effort bring tangible results, their intrinsic motivation increases and they come to understand that the goal setting and planning process is the secret for achieving whatever they want in life.

Planning can be done regardless of your pedagogical practice, including in a traditional classroom. Just make sure you have units of study that speak to learners and review with them the units for the week. Knowing what they must accomplish is critical to developing a plan to tackle the units. Practice coaching learners to plan small goals and continue this practice until they can plan their month. You can discuss coaching strategies with others by joining our online community, the link to which can be found easily on our website: BecomingEinsteinsTeacher.com.

~ UNITS OF STUDY ~

A unit of study supports students in their learning process by using Relational Learning Steps 2–5, as previously discussed. Its structure is aligned to the brain's learning system and allows you to incorporate practices of project-based learning, personalized learning, competency-based learning, blended learning, and autonomous learning. The objective is to develop the required cognitive control to form nonhackable and creative beings, enabling students to live a fulfilling life.

By breaking down the learning process, learners will understand they can learn anything. This results in the opportunity to improve a new skill and form good habits. Units of study may have a duration of 3 to 10 days. In our experience, students learn which time of the day they are mostly productive in certain subjects. The unit's time frame allows them to be productive on that time of the day. It makes sense. For instance, I prefer to work on activities that involve writing early in the morning and I can work on anything related to numbers any time of the day. I meet with school leaders at different times of the week or participate in a conference from time to time. I distribute tasks over several days. As learners get to know themselves, they will get their own activities done when they are most productive.

A productive unit of study taps into the natural way that human brains work and ensures the right balance of neurotransmitters by connecting learners' passions to the curriculum.

~ A SAMPLE UNIT OF STUDY AND ITS STEPS ~

This is what a music unit of study might look like:

1. ***Explore***

   During this step, ask students to reflect on the theme and state their preexisting knowledge. Daily experience, everyday life, expectations, questions, doubts, and curiosity become the starting point for this exploration. Students may respond to a contextualized question or hypothesize what they will learn and achieve in the unit.

Typical questions would include: Can you list some music genres? Who created them? Why? Can you associate a singer or band to each genre? What genres do you enjoy? What are your favorite singers or bands? Why do you like them? What would it take for you to like samba?

2. *Research*

In this step, students research new information about the unit of study through visual sources (books, reports), audio (audiobooks), audiovisual sources (videos), dialogue, interviews, or direct meetings. Researching the new information leads to the development of a knowledge base, which becomes apparent through the analysis that the student is required to complete.

Encourage students to seek their sources based on the things they enjoy. You will increase the likelihood of the students understanding the concept. For example, if a student is learning music and loves soccer, encourage him to explore what happens to a soccer match when fans start chanting the team's song. Give him the freedom to express himself, and you will see wonders.

3. *Practice*

This step includes planned activities you provide or those suggested by learners as they gain learning autonomy. You may enrich practice with project-based learning during this step, evoking problem solving, creativity, and critical thinking, which are all part of competency-based learning. As learners grow in their ability to propose new activities, their learning autonomy will increase.

Activities in a music unit might include writing a song, sharing a collection of preferred genres, or writing an essay about the history of the learner's favorite band.

4. *Relate*

   During this step, students realize the real purpose of the unit by relating what they have learned to their own lives through activities and personal reflections. The most successful approaches help students find **purpose and meaning in what they are learning.**

Get to know learners each time you interact with them. Take notes about their aspirations, likes, and dislikes. Make sure you motivate them to relate their learning to what you know about them. Incorporate questions that help them do so. Here are a few examples for a music unit: Have you changed your music preferences after this unit? Can you relate each genre to how it makes you feel? Can you match your moods to a certain genre? What genre would you recommend to your friends?

~ HOW TO MOVE STUDENTS THROUGH UNITS OF STUDY ~

Units of study must always speak to the student. It is okay to work with a group of students together at the same pace. Nevertheless, make sure you allow them to explore the unit themselves, at their own pace, once they feel ready to do so. Or, you may move little by little toward a personalized approach, allowing students to advance individually at their own pace.

Make sure you have additional units ready for learners who move more quickly. In our experience, learners take two to three months to understand the process, and once they do, they will want more units and will learn faster than you may expect.

Once students finish a unit of study, they must present their learning to their educators in a one-to-one setting whenever possible. Even if they present as a group, each student must share their individual work. This process will develop presentation skills and demonstrate learning: their approach to each learning step, their findings, why they selected certain resources, how they organized knowledge, how they developed each practical activity, and finally, how they will use the new knowledge in their lives. Give freedom to learners to express what they have learned. It will foster creativity. You can check out units of study on our website, BecomingEinsteinsTeacher.com, as examples to get you started.

Here is a practice for you: Develop a unit of study for a theme of your choice using the learning process in this chapter. Then, personalize it to Mary, a student you perceive as apathetic and lacking motivation or interest. Using the unit of study you created and personalized, how could you incorporate some of the learning approaches? Join our Facebook discussion group to ask questions and share your experience!

~ THE ORGANIZATIONAL GRID—HELPING LEARNERS SYNTHESIZE NEW KNOWLEDGE ~

Learning products depend on the learner's ability to synthesize information, and their outcomes can vary. Still, clear evidence must exist that the learner understands the unit of study. We strongly recommend the use of organizational grids (also known as org grids), which help learners synthesize new knowledge. In our practice, the introduction of org grids increased students' reading comprehension by an average of 40% per year. Org grids are a powerful reading and comprehension tool.

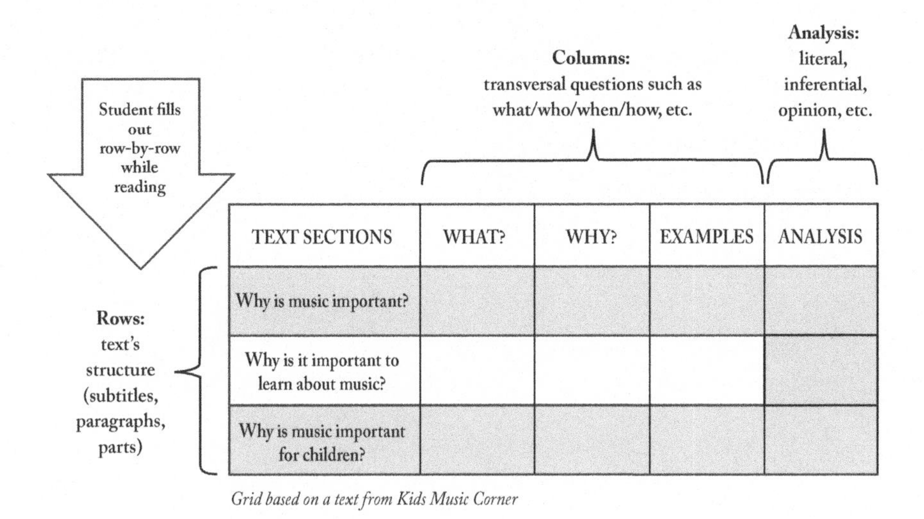

Grid based on a text from Kids Music Corner

Figure 11.3: Example of an Organizational Grid

The elements of an org grid:

- **Rows**: correspond to the text's structure—the titles of the segments to be read;
- **Columns**: correspond to functional aspects, with questions like who, what, where, when, why, and how; and
- **Far right column**: always a transversal question that requires some level of analysis. It can be literal, such as: "What does the text say?" It can be inferential, such as: "What would I have added to this text? What do I think the text should say? What may be implied by the text?" It can express an opinion, such as: "What do I feel about this topic?"

Learners fill out the grid one row at a time, as they read a text from start to finish, and synthesize the information in their own words while they read. Once this process is complete, learners may create a concept map, which will show their understanding of the subject. For more information on how to create a concept map,[75] please visit our website, at BecomingEinsteinsTeacher.com. Concept maps make it easier to recall anything you've learned.

CHAPTER 12

EXECUTION MODE

"A student is not a vessel to be filled,
but a torch to be kindled."

~PLUTARCH

In the Discovery Channel series *MythBusters: The Search*, host Kyle Hill challenges science-savvy contenders to bust myths. In one episode, participants had to ride a rigged bike for 12 feet. Not a big deal, except for the catch: When the rider turned the handlebar to the right, the front wheel would move to the left, and vice-versa. It sounds simple if you pay triple attention to the left-right turn. Well, six out of six contenders were unable to ride the bike for 12 feet.

Riding the rigged bike is a challenge because we already have neural networks in our brains that determine our automatic reactions when riding a bike. We want to move the handlebar to the right when going right, and to the left when going left. Brain conflict like this happens whenever we want to learn anything that deviates from our already established neural networks, or habits already ingrained in our brains. It is difficult, but not impossible.

At the end of the *MythBusters* episode, Hill explained that the reversed-handlebar bike can be used only with "*a lot* of practice." With a clear understanding of how the bike works and lots of practice, riders can master the reversed-handlebar. Hill himself became an expert on riding the rigged bike and now has a challenge riding a "normal" bike. He formed new bike-riding neural networks.

The same goes for putting into practice an approach to learning where students are in charge: It requires rewiring the brain, and it will take practice. Autonomous learning does not happen like magic just because you are using new tools. Becoming an autonomous learner is a process, which requires continuous guided practice. With that in mind, Relational Learning incorporates a scale of learning autonomy, which determines what types of support students need from their teachers.

~ THE FOUR LEVELS OF AUTONOMY IN THE RELATIONAL LEARNING FRAMEWORK ~

Perhaps one of the greatest reasons for the Relational Learning Framework's effectiveness is its distinct levels of autonomy. You learned in the previous chapters how to use the six steps of the Relational Learning Framework and its tools to develop your students' potential.

Throughout this book, we have reinforced that Relational Learning starts from where your students are. A true learning experience invokes personal discovery, which fosters intrinsic motivation and student agency. There are two questions to answer at this point:

1. How do you know your students are autonomous learners?

2. How to support your students in their autonomous learning development?

Learning to walk is a process. Learning to ride a bike is a process. Learning to speak a new language is a process. Learning to learn is also a process. Because of that, we established four levels of autonomy students move through, each of which requires a different level of support from teachers. Thus, while students are using the six-step Relational Learning Framework, teachers are providing the necessary support to enhance their skills.

Let's start by understanding the levels of learning autonomy and how to identify which level each of your students is at:

1. **Guided Level**

   In this level, students are learning techniques to self-govern and self-organize, and require precise guidance toward the achievement of their goals. At this level, teachers provide students with a clear framework to follow.

   Students learn to set short-term goals focused on specific activities. It is at this level that their behavior responds to consequences: to avoid punishment (for example: *I won't hit my classmate because if I do I'll get punished)* or to obtain a prize (for example: *I do my homework because if I do it my parents will buy me a scooter).*

2. **Advised Level**

   Within the second level of autonomy, students' behavior still depends on external rules, but is carried out in line with an established order that students are beginning to recognize and follow. It is here that they begin to understand a rule as a functional structure that everyone participates in, where the models of authority are present as guides and companions in the process, not as imposing figures.

This level works with a mediated communication process—a continuous conversation between the teacher and the student to align expectations and accomplishments. Students will still choose behaviors in order to satisfy others (*I have to be good so my parents feel proud of me*) or to maintain a social group (*I have to do this the way my friends tell me to, as we all act the same*).

3. **Oriented Level**

   This is a transition level, in which students are demonstrating whether their skills are sufficiently developed to function under the parameters of the autonomous level. They are able to go through most units of study with minimum guidance, and present visible improvements in the quality of their deliverables, identification of personal interests, skill development, and self-assessment. Students can set goals and plan months ahead, and have the intrinsic motivation to complete their plans.

4. **Autonomous Level**

   Students are autonomous when they are fully self-managed, and learning dynamics are products of an agreement between student and educator. The basis for achieving this level of autonomy is when the learner's actions are motivated by values and acceptance. They follow rules because there is a clear consensus about their usefulness, rather than because they have been imposed.

~ ASSESSING PROGRESS IN THE PROCESS ~

Now it is time to put it all together. First, develop your units of study using the six-step Relational Learning Framework. In each interaction you have with your students, you can personalize each learner's experience by updating activities and allowing them to choose which ones they want to work on.

The next step is to assess progress in the process using the four levels of autonomy. Because you are now aware of the skills being developed within the learning process you designed, your guidance will improve these skills in each interaction. You no longer question the learner with the aim of assessing their rigid disciplinary knowledge, but from a place of encouraging student exploration. This means asking exploratory questions, both cognitive and experiential, that lead students to seek answers in a self-paced learning process.

Here is how to support students in their learning autonomy development:

LEVEL 1—GUIDED LEARNERS

Start by making sure learners are planning correctly, with small goals, and ask questions to help them self-assess their progress. The self-assessment is done in each step at this level.

Questions you might ask in the Guided Learning stage:

- How do you feel?
- How long did it take?
- Were your goals clear? Have you used more or less time than you allotted to this task?

Remember students are learning the learning process. They may hesitate to answer these questions at first, but doing so will eventually become a habit. You must provide guidance to students after each step, to ensure they get the process right. Focus on the process, not the content. As they learn the process, you are enabling them to learn anything. It is like when you learn to ride the bike: you can go anywhere you want.

Give learners one thing to focus on in the next unit of study, such as improving their answers on the org grid (see chapter 11). Praise the progress in the process! You help learners assess each step of the way because they need small wins to start feeding their "I-can-do-this" attitude. You are helping them build intrinsic motivation and perseverance.

LEVEL 2—ADVISED LEARNERS

Once learners feel more comfortable with the process and can go through any two steps of the Relational Learning Framework without teachers' help, challenge them to increase the number of activities they include in their plan to complete their goals, and continue to support their self-assessment. Make sure they see their own progress, which increases self-esteem and intrinsic motivation.

Allow learners to work through two learning steps before presenting them to you. If learners have understood the concepts presented and have done the activities well, they can move forward to the next learning step. This is important, as you are helping learners reach their excellence level and have the immediate chance to correct their course if the learner has not understood the concepts. Praise their effort to challenge themselves. Give them one thing to focus on in the next stage of learning or the next unit of study.

LEVEL 3—ORIENTED LEARNERS

Learners are now planning their days effortlessly and can finish the activities of two to three complete learning steps within their budgeted time frame. You can then move one step forward and guide learners to finding a solution for a question or issue they do not understand. You become the person who makes it possible for learners to answer their own questions and solve their own problems. You are the facilitator of the learning process. Ask questions; do not give answers. Encourage them to find the answers.

Challenge learners to set goals for a full month, distributing all activities within this time frame, as they have a clear understanding of their pacing capacity by now. Intrinsic motivation starts to flourish. Continue to review daily planning and help learners assess whether they are on track at the end of each week. Remember to always praise the effort learners put into the tasks, not how smart or intelligent they are.

LEVEL 4—AUTONOMOUS LEARNERS

By now, learners are able to complete one full unit of study and present it to you, including a description of the process used to complete the unit of study and how they will use it in their lives. Conduct conversations with learners to support them in recognizing ways to deepen their understanding and acknowledge areas in need of improvement. Learners will begin inquiring about the materials and resources needed to achieve their goals.

Encourage learners to share their progress, difficulties, challenges, and strengths. The learner knows best what needs to be improved and how to do so with the external support necessary for their growth. Imagine you are training a runner for a major competition. You cannot compete and run as their coach. The runner is the one who needs to train and perform. So it is for your students.

Explore what learners are thinking of their future. By now, intrinsic motivation is well established, and learners believe they can achieve anything they set their minds to.

When learners have agency, it becomes innate for them to:

- set challenging and achievable goals;
- develop strategies to reach those goals;
- follow a specific learning process and learn anything with a purpose;
- self-assess their progress;
- find meaning in what they learn; and
- relate what they learn to their lives;

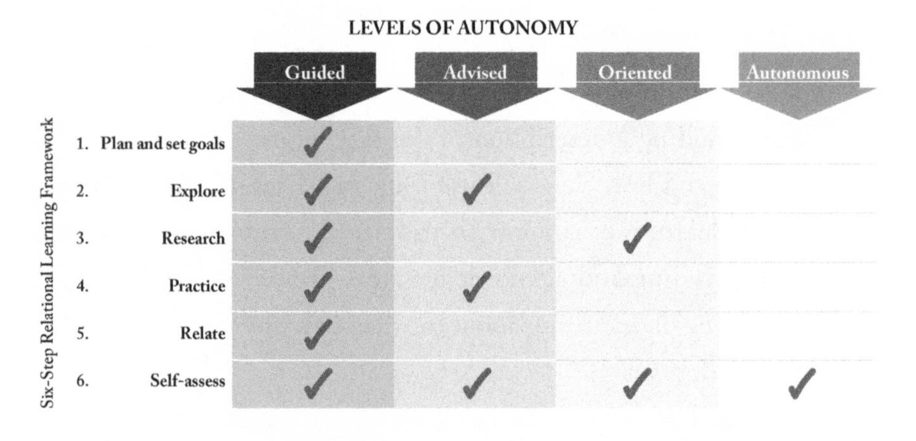

Figure 12.1: Teacher support required in each level of autonomy

~ THE MOST FREQUENTLY ASKED QUESTION ~

Once educators start using the Relational Learning tools and see their students' progress through the levels of autonomy, the most frequently asked question surfaces: How do I provide personalized attention to each of my 30 students within a limited period of time?

If you have many years of teaching experience, most likely you are used to lecturing, assigning homework, and testing. When using the Relational Learning Framework, you no longer use this process. Students learn with the units of study you previously prepared, and you provide the necessary support while they work on each unit. Students will be in different steps of the framework or even different units at the same time. Therefore, they don't need the kind of group attention you used to provide.

In a given day, you may work with 5 or 10 students during your time together, monitoring their progress in the units according to their level of autonomy. The remaining 20 to 25 students continue working independently, at the learning pace they require. What really matters is students' overall progress in your subject.

The more you personalize each student's experience, the more intrinsically motivated they will be to accomplish 100% of your units. That is why it is worth learning this new approach. When you work one-on-one with your students, you get to know them really well and discover what matters to them, what motivates them, and what triggers learning for them. Your goal is to help your students become autonomous learners, while you coach them to fulfill their potential. The more autonomous they become, the less support they need.

You may ask, Does this mean I am now irrelevant? On the contrary—you become even more relevant because your students need guidance to explore their greatness! Remember: Their experience with you is the perfect opportunity to try, fail, and try again, until they are ready for life. The more your students practice learning under the Relational Learning Framework, the more they will be prepared to be anyone they want to be in life.

Rejoice when students start learning faster. Like a raving football fan who believes they won the game as much as the players, celebrate with learners for each of their achievements!

CHAPTER 13

BECOMING EINSTEIN'S TEACHER

"I pushed the limit and I found it."

–Luke Durbridge

It happened in 1939. University of California, Berkeley, doctoral student George Dantzig was late for a statistics lecture. He just had time to take note of the two statistics problems on the blackboard before the class adjourned. Dantzig had an undergraduate degree in mathematics and physics by 1936, and received his master's degree in mathematics in 1938. Math problems were simple for him. Nevertheless, it took him a few days to find the solution to these homework problems, as they were a little harder than usual. Perhaps this challenge was a consequence of him missing the class during which the problems were discussed.

Dantzig turned in the solution for both problems directly to the office of the professor, Dr. Jerzy Neyman, profoundly sorry for the overdue assignment. After all, Neyman was his doctoral advisor and Dantzig had been disrespectful in being late for class. In the end, his extremely late arrival played in his favor: Dantzig had no idea that those two problems were unproven statistical theorems, not an assignment! He had worked on them for a couple of days and solved them. No one ever told Dantzig it was impossible to do so.[76]

Since then, this episode in Dantzig's life has become a motivational lesson in positive thinking, the belief we are capable of doing anything. I would have loved to hear Neyman's side of the story too. How many times did the professor guide and motivate Dantzig to explore his passion for math? How many times did he lock eyes with Dantzig to say, "I believe in you," before dismissing the student on his way to continue his work? Can you imagine how Neyman felt when he saw his student's solutions to the supposedly unsolvable equations? He had a genius attending his classes!

How would you like to have a Dantzig, Einstein, Phelps, Earhart, Curie, Edison, Jobs, and so many other geniuses learning under your guidance? Like any human being, these were not perfect students. However, they had one thing in common: an intrinsic motivation that burned inside them and made them pursue their dreams.

Within the Relational Learning Framework, students learn to work like PhDs from a young age: They have a hypothesis, research it, practice it, and apply it to their lives. They are autonomous learners with a clear learning pathway that they set for themselves. Their teachers are advisors who guide them throughout the learning process to reach what they want in life.

Now, reflect with me on this: The United States has 56.4 million students in K-12 alone.[77] Imagine if these children were using the Relational Learning Framework, capable of asking questions, researching, collaborating, prototyping, and finding solutions for current problems that they have identified and are passionate about. These are problems like transportation, housing, healthcare, workforce development, international relations, and so many more.

Imagine if teachers believed in each learner's capacity to innovate, regardless of their age, erasing the word "impossible" from their dictionary forever. If a 4-year-old asks an average of 300 questions a day, wouldn't this be an ideal age at which to start exploring new perspectives for a current problem? Perhaps we could have already found the cure for cancer, the solution for pollution, and the end of hunger.

Can you imagine a school system where 56.4 million students create patented products and solutions daily? Where they often collaborate with other students whom they have never met before because they use the same learning process? What could happen to the country's economy? Most of all, can you imagine the level of satisfaction, productivity, and motivation of a generation with these opportunities?

I believe all students can be, do, and have anything they desire. I believe they can learn efficiently when we tap into the number one resource they all have: a brain! I believe learners are unstoppable when they find their intrinsic motivation. We already have plenty of examples of students' capabilities around the world. Nineteen-year-old Boyan Slat created a device to collect plastic from the ocean.[78] He aims to clean all oceans by 2050. Impacted by the Flint Water crisis, 11-year-old Gitanjali Rao invented an inexpensive lead-detecting device to prevent anyone else from getting sick.[79] Leroy Mwasaru was just 17 when he invented a human waste bioreactor that transformed fecal material into clean cooking fuel to be used in kitchens.[80]

"You're born an original, don't die a copy."

–**John Mason**

I was once in a meeting with 15 ministers of education from different countries, discussing the use of technology in the classroom. I emphasized the importance of a pedagogical strategy and teacher-readiness to ensure the success of any national program using technology. Laura, a 15-year-old student at that time, accompanied me and shared with the ministers the difference that the Relational Learning Framework had made in her learning, choices, behavior, and emotions. Among many interesting questions, the ministers asked her how she felt having students of different ages learning with her in the same space. She answered, "You are with 14 other ministers here, learning something that interests you all. You are not the same age, or even from the same country! Why can't we have the same experience in school?"

I am optimistic that we will eventually have schools that fit learners, instead of learners having to fit schools. School will be a place where students discover what they want in life, and build a strong foundation to enable them to realize their potential on their own terms. These schools will let go of comparison and focus on continuous refinement of learners' skills with a definite purpose. Perhaps the answer for Bloom's 2-sigma problem is children teaching and learning from each other with the support of teachers, a viable alternative to one-to-one tutoring. School then becomes a collective intelligence that enhances biological intelligence, like the internet is a collective intelligence that enhances artificial intelligence.

Throughout the last decade, I've witnessed how children yearn to control their destiny, to do what they love, and to have flexibility. These opportunities are more important to most of them than high pay. Perhaps that's why so many more people are becoming freelancers, taking on contract-based jobs with flexibility in time, high-quality work requirements, self-management, and that require practical knowledge of finance, legal, sales, and marketing. In 2019, there was a 78% increase in the total earnings of freelancers in the U.S., and 34% of U.S. workers had done some amount of freelancing.[81]

The school Einstein loved treated him as an individual, respected his personal traits, required no memorization or repetition, fostered independent thinking and responsibility, and linked learning to each student's passion. Throughout his life, Einstein tended to disrespect authority figures, mostly teachers. Nevertheless, in the cantonal school he loved them! It is clear now why he did.

"'It's impossible,' said pride.
'It's risky,' said experience.
'It's pointless,' said reason.
'Give it a try,' whispered the heart."

–UNKNOWN

Dr. Albert Bandura concluded back in 1986: "People who develop their competencies, self-regulatory skills, and enabling beliefs in their efficacy can generate a wider array of options that expand their freedom of action, and are more successful in realizing desired futures than those with less developed agentic resources."[82] In other words, people with a high level of autonomy will be whoever they want in life.

The Relational Learning Framework offers a path to transition from traditional schooling to a school with the sole purpose of fostering the highest level of human achievement. The framework can coexist with today's curriculum and grading requirements. It can also be used in school settings that are evolving into new models. Does this sound impossible? It is not. Between the possible and impossible is an effective process – the Relational Learning Framework makes a new kind of learning possible within today's school systems.

At this point, you have two choices. Choice number one is to do nothing. If you do nothing with the information you've learned in this book, what will you get? Nothing. Choice number two is to take a leap of faith, start using the Relational Learning Framework with your students, and see it working for you. Even if it only does HALF of what I've claimed in this book, your effort of practicing what you learned is paid for as soon as your students start using Step 1 on their own!

Do you think you could be successful if you followed the Relational Learning Framework? Imagine this scenario: You used what I showed you in Steps 1 and 2 and got your students to clearly understand what they are capable of and to learn from their own starting point. Then you applied what I shared in Steps 3 and 4, got your students excited about finding the resources aligned with what they love, and saw them develop the soft skills that will benefit them for life. Then you used Steps 5 and 6 and got your students to solve problems on their own, using what they had just learned, and now see they have higher self-esteem, perseverance, and accountability. Let me ask you the more important question: Do you think your students will love learning, become self-starters, develop intrinsic motivation and learning autonomy, and succeed in life as a result?

I want you to think about that one student you have who is struggling right now and would benefit the most from your application of what you've learned in this book. How much would it be worth to you if that one student suddenly found their passion for learning and never had trouble learning ever again? How much would it be worth to that student? Now multiply that by all of the students you teach and influence every single day.

I believe you got to the end of this book because you have a burning desire to never stop growing. You have a calling to develop human potential. I believe the ones privileged to be in your classroom are meant to be there in this very moment. These students could be in any other school, or classroom, or household. But you know what? They are in yours. You are tasked and privileged to develop that human potential in front of you right now.

I have worked with teachers, leaders, and parents in rural and urban schools, with and without technology, around tight curriculums and grading systems, poor and rich. So many teachers and education leaders with fewer resources may have said, "This framework works for rich students, not ours." Instead, they were humbled to learn and figure out how to apply it with their students. Figuring it out may take a while until all the practices are in place, but once it happens, the results are unimaginable!

Each step of this practice is increasing your students' chance of success because you are discovering a systematic framework to make it happen. This is how you fulfill your calling. This is how you develop human potential. This very moment can be the highlight of your career, the finest realization in your life. It matters to you and to me, but most of all, it matters to learners and to the world. So light up your spark, find your voice, and become the educator that learners need now. Let's get to work.

Here are a few first steps:

1. Plan to build from where you are—not to wipe it away and start new;

2. Reconnect with your own passion and remember a time when learning excited you;

3. Invest in continuous, relevant professional development;

4. Set aside preconceived notions of the resources required for student success and resolve to try something new;

5. Start your students with Step 1: Goal Setting and Planning; and

6. Focus on progress, not perfection.

Each day, I am grateful for the teachers already enabling leaners to reach their highest potential. They are genuinely committed to being better tomorrow than they are today. They see the possibilities in their minds, have the courage to take action, and experience their students enjoying deeper, more effective learning. They understand the destination is important, but the meaning learners give to the journey is even more important.

This is my invitation to every member of the education community: Humbly submit to the task of understanding the Relational Learning Framework and putting it to use in your classrooms—embrace growing from where you and your students are right now.

Your experience and training brought you to this point and provided the foundation for your advancement. Build on it by improving the learning process. Listen to what your heart is saying right now and take action. Take one simple step at a time and enjoy small wins each day to get you to the destination you yearn for. This is your life's work, your mark in this world. Commit to be your best, not just to do your best. You are enabling your students to do the same—to each becoming Einstein in their own way.

ACKNOWLEDGMENTS

"Gratitude is the ultimate state of receivership."

–**Dr. Joe Dispenza**

This work started with years of writing articles and having my beloved husband Brian editing them, until I was prepared to write a book. I am grateful for my life's journey up to now, and for the ones I worked and interacted with along the way, which got me ready to this point of sharing these words with you.

Thanks to Dr. Bena Kallick, a renowned author herself, for the encouragement and motivation to write this book. A huge thank you to my team at Learning One to One, as this work would be impossible without them. Thank you to my dear friends and first reviewers, who sincerely shared their opinion about the manuscript and supported me on this journey of continuous improvement: Amy Anderson, Jerry Haar, Carol Carter, German Escorcia, Barbara Bibas Montero, William Burdette, Judy Perez, Leonardo Garnier, Virginia Emmons, Marcelo Cabrol, Terry Torok, Chip Lunsford, and Sergio Godinho. A big thank you to my dear friends Ania Rodriguez and Renee Lopez-Cantera for their technical advices.

My infinite gratitude to the thousands of teachers whom I had the honor to work with and inspired me throughout the years. Special thanks to the teachers who shared their stories for this book: Ashley Delgado,

Nicole Warner, Pauline Yoshizumi, Milton Nettles, and Chanel Williams. A special thanks to Kristi Oda for her support.

Thanks to MLS (Major League Soccer) for assigning my husband to referee weekend games. I used this alone time wisely to work on this book.

My gratitude to my family, whose love is my inspiration to be a better person each day. My infinite love and gratitude to my husband Brian, my biggest supporter and cheerleader, with whom life is the greatest adventure.

Looking forward, my heart is filled with gratitude for the teachers, leaders, and parents this book will inspire, and for the students' lives it will touch. May this be my ultimate state of receivership.

ABOUT THE AUTHOR

Erika Twani is a learning enthusiast and an optimist focused on a better world built by humans with practical skills and life purpose. She is the cofounder and CEO of the Learning One to One, where, along with experts, she explores ways to foster human achievement through Relational Learning. The framework is based on applied neuroscience, psychology, philosophy, pedagogy, and technology. Her philosophy is to simplify complex concepts and make them useful for everyone, starting with children.

Erika has advised government officials and education leaders around the world on the use of technology in education, has written various articles on the topic, and has worked with public and private schools to guide the practical use of Relational Learning. She led Learning One to One into five countries in the first year alone, touching the lives of more than 100,000 students.

Before co-founding Learning One to One, Erika was Microsoft's education industry director for Multi-Country Americas. Under her leadership, the company's Partners in Learning program enabled 90,000 teachers per year in technology, in addition to sales and marketing. Prior to that, she worked in the technology giant's Unlimited Potential Group, helping technology reach underserved communities worldwide, for which Microsoft awarded her with its Circle of Excellence. Erika also worked at Oracle before Microsoft and founded and ran her own technology company before Oracle.

Innovation in learning usually happens in silos, and Erika wants to empower educators to bring it out of these silos and scale it. To do this, she uses insights, skills, and experience from 20+ years of experience working with corporate technology companies, which enabled her to shape products and services for worldwide scalability. Erika's corporate experience has given her a clear understanding of large organizations' challenges to motivate employees, foster creativity, and create long-lasting relationships with customers and partners, regardless of their locations.

Corporations benefit from the same principles identified in Erika's work, as they implement simple learning and skill development processes that contribute to individuals' personal growth, intrinsic motivation, and life purpose. Consequently, individual achievement results in the organization's success.

Besides being an author, Erika is also an international speaker, adviser, avid reader, and adventurer. Most of all, she is a learner, committed to investing 20% of her time in learning. Her organization serves schools and institutions worldwide with professional development, consulting services, and education technology. She has a B.S. in software engineering and an MBA in entrepreneurship. She also sits on various boards. Erika lives in Fort Lauderdale, Florida, USA, with her husband, Brian.

REFERENCES

CHAPTER 1

1. Isaacson, W. 2007. *Einstein: His Life and Universe.* New York, NY: Simon & Schuster.

2. Carl Sagan Interview at TVO. Accessed November 3, 2020. https://www.youtube.com/watch?v=acBRahW5c-A.

3. Steinberg, L. 1996. *Beyond the Classroom.* New York, NY: Simon & Schuster.

4. Kun-Hsing MD, Y.; Miron, O.; Wilf-Miron, R.; et al. 2019. *Suicide Rates Among Adolescents and Young Adults in the United States, 2000–2017.* Research Letter, June 18, 2019. JAMA Network.

   Curtin MA, S. C.; Heron, M. 2019. *Death Rates Due to Suicide and Homicide Among Persons Aged 10–24: United States, 2000–2017.* NCHS Data Brief, No. 352, October 2019.

   American Foundation for Suicide Prevention. Suicide Statistics. Accessed on November 3, 2020. https://afsp.org/suicide-statistics/

5. De Guimps, R. 1890. *Pestalozzi, His Life and Work.* New York, NY: D. Appleton and Company.

6. Isaacson, W. 2007. *Einstein: His Life and Universe.* New York, NY: Simon & Schuster.

CHAPTER 2

7. Horace, Epistles, II, 2, 187–189.

8. Galton, F. 1869. *Hereditary Genius: An Inquiry Into Its Laws and Consequences.* London: Macmillan and Co.

9. Wolf, T. H. 1973. *Alfred Binet.* Chicago, IL: The University of Chicago Press.

10. Spektorowski, A.; Ireni-Saban, L. 2013. *Politics of Eugenics: Productionism, Population, and National Welfare.* London: Routledge.

11. Cox Miles, C.; Terman, L. M. 1926. *Genetic Studies of Genius. Vol. 2: The Early Mental Traits of 300 Geniuses.* Stanford, CA: Stanford University Press.

12. Wechsler, D. 1939. *The Measurement of Adult Intelligence* (First Ed.). Baltimore, MD: Williams & Witkins.

13. Jarman, B.; Land, G. 1993. *Breakpoint and Beyond: Mastering the Future Today.* New York, NY: HarperBusiness.

14. Harlow, J. M.; Massachusetts Medical Society. 1869. *Recovery from the Passage of an Iron Bar through the Head.* Boston: David Clapp & Son.
    Bigelow, H. J. 1850. *Dr. Harlow's Case of Recovery from the Passage of an Iron Bar through the Head.* London: American Journal of the Medical Sciences. 20 n.s. (39): 13–22.

15. Davitz, J. R.; Beldoch, M.; Blau, S. 1964. *The Communication of Emotional Meaning,* New York, NY: McGraw-Hill.

16. Goleman, D. 2005. *Emotional Intelligence.* New York, NY: Penguin Random House.

17. Goleman, D. 2005. *Emotional Intelligence.* New York, NY: Penguin Random House.
    Bradberry, T.; Greaves, J. 2009. *Emotional Intelligence 2.0.* San Diego, CA: TalentSmart.

18. Durlak, J.; Weissberg, R. P.; Dymnicki, A. B.; Taylor, R. D.; Schellinger, 2011. *The Impact of Enhancing Students' Social and Emotional Learning: A*

Meta-Analysis of School-Based Universal Interventions. Journal of Experiential Education. Volume 34 Issue 2.

Van Rooy, D.; Viswesvaran, C. 2004. *Emotional intelligence: A meta-analytic investigation of predictive validity and nomological net.* Journal of Vocational Behavior. 65 (1): 71–95.

19. Muro, M.; Whiton, J.; Maxim, R. 2019. *What Jobs are Affected by AI?* Metropolitan Policy Program at Brookings Institute.
20. Hanushek, E. A.; Jamison, D. T.; Jamison, E. A.; Woessmann, L. 2008. *Education and Economic Growth.* Education Next, Spring 2008.

CHAPTER 3

21. Podolsky, A.; Kini, T.; Bishop, J.; Darling-Hammond, L. 2016. *Solving the Teacher Shortage: How to Attract and Retain Excellent Educators.* Palo Alto, CA: Learning Policy Institute.
22. Hussar, W. J.; Bailey, T. M. 2020. *Projections of Education Statistics to 2028.* National Center for Education Statistics. Accessed on November 3, 2020. https://nces.ed.gov/pubsearch/pubsinfo.asp?pubid=2020024.

CHAPTER 4

23. Isaacson, W. 2007. *Einstein: His Life and Universe.* New York, NY: Simon & Schuster.
24. Dispenza, J. 2008. *Evolve Your Brain: The Science of Changing Your Mind.* Deerfield Beach, FL: Health Communications, Inc.
25. Bedell, G. 2016. *Teenage Mental-Health Crisis: Rates of Depression Have Soared in Past 25 Years.* Independent, February 27, 2016.
26. Fleming, S. 2019. *This is the World's Biggest Mental Health Problem—and You Might not Have Heard of It.* World Economic Forum, January 14, 2019.

Mental health in the workplace. 2019. World Economic Forum. Accessed on November 3, 2020. https://www.who.int/mental_health/in_the_workplace/en/

27. Dispenza, J. 2008. *Evolve Your Brain: The Science of Changing Your Mind.* Deerfield Beach, FL: Health Communications, Inc.

Heron, M. 2019. *Deaths: Leading Causes for 2017.* U.S. Department of Health and Human Services, Centers for Disease Control and Prevention, National Center for Health Statistics, National Vital Statistics System. National Statistics Reports, Volume 68, No. 6.

Celano M.D., C.; Villegas M.D., A.; Albanese B.A., A.; Gaggin M.D., M.P.H., H.; Huffman M.D., J. 2019. *Depression and Anxiety in Heart Failure: a Review.* Harv Rev Psychiatry. 2018 Jul-Aug; 26(4): 175–184.

28. *Mental health in the workplace.* 2019. World Economic Forum. Accessed on November 3, 2020. https://www.who.int/mental_health/in_the_workplace/en/

29. Bonfanti, L.; Parolisi, R.; La Rosa, C. 2020. *Brain Structural Plasticity: From Adult Neurogenesis to Immature Neurons.* Frontiers in Neuroscience, February 4, 2020.

30. Dweck, C. 2006. *Mindset: The New Psychology of Success.* New York, NY: Random House Publishing Group.

31. Bandura, A. 1986. *Social Foundations of Thought and Action: A Social Cognitive Theory.* Englewood Cliffs, N.J.: Prentice-Hall.

Bandura, A. 2008. *Social cognitive theory of mass communication. In J. Bryant & M. B. Oliver (Eds.), Media Effects: Advances in Theory and Research* (pp. 94–124). New York, NY: Routledge.

Bandura, A. 1993. *Perceived Self-Efficacy in Cognitive Development and Functioning.* Educational Psychologist. 28 (2): 117–148.

Bandura, A., ed. 1995. "Frontmatter." Frontmatter. *In Self-Efficacy in Changing Societies, i-iv.* Cambridge: Cambridge University Press.

CHAPTER 5

32. Hanna Barbera's *The Jetson's* episode. Accessed on November 3, 2020. https://www.youtube.com/watch?v=EjSEvriQmgw&list=PLXeLD1jAJhNhwejkud1GedCgj_ewRIE2Y&index=2

33. Dispenza, J. 2008. *Evolve Your Brain: The Science of Changing Your Mind.* Deerfield Beach, FL: Health Communications, Inc.
Duhigg, C. 2014. *The Power of Habit: Why We Do What We Do in Life and Business.* New York, NY: Random House.
Polk, T. A. 2018. *The Learning Brain.* The Great Courses.

34. Dispenza, J. 2008. *Evolve Your Brain: The Science of Changing Your Mind.* Deerfield Beach, FL: Health Communications, Inc.
Kotulak, R. 1997. *Inside the Brain: Revolutionary discoveries of how the mind works.* Kansas City, KS: Andrews McMeel Publishing.

35. *Scrabble Classique de Compétition.* Accessed on November 3, 2020. https://www.fisf.net/competitions/scrabble-classique.html

36. Rand, D.; Cohen, J. 2017. *The Rise and Fall of Cognitive Control.* Behavioral Scientist Magazine, July 7, 2017.

37. Duhigg, C. 2014. *The Power of Habit: Why We Do What We Do in Life and Business.* New York, NY: Random House.
McGonigal, K. 2011. *The Willpower Instinct: How Self-Control Works, Why It Matters, and What You Can Do To Get More of It.* New York, NY: Penguin Group.

38. Aristizabal, P. 2018. *Educación Aumentada en la Era de la Exponencialidad.* Buenos Aires, Argentina.

39. Costa, A.; Kallick, B. 2008. *Learning and Leading with Habits of Mind: 16 essential characteristics for success.* Alexandria, VA: ASCD.

40. Reference: 7 hours a day, 200 days a year, for 12 years equals 16,800 hours.

41. Albert Einstein used to say that related to science, with a little tweak. It comes from the Bible Romans 8:19 "For the creation waits with eager longing for the revealing **of the** sons of **God.**"

CHAPTER 6

42. Sanders, R. 2016. *'Neural Dust' Could Treat the Body from Inside.* University of California, Berkeley. Accessed on November 3, 2020. https://www.universityofcalifornia.edu/news/neural-dust-could-treat-body-inside.

43. Matthews, C. 2017. *Spending on AI to Reach $46 Billion in 2020.* Axios, Economy & Business, April 19, 2017. Accessed on November 3, 2020. https://www.axios.com/spending-on-ai-to-reach-46-billion-in-2020-1513301689-a3c07136-46be-47a5-8e95-6e7c4725939d.html

Hupfer, S.; Jarvis, D.; Loucks, J.; Murphy, T. 2019. *Future in the Balance? How Countries Are Pursuing an AI Advantage.* Deloitte Insights, May 1, 2019. Accessed on November 3, 2020. https://www2.deloitte.com/us/en/insights/focus/cognitive-technologies/ai-investment-by-country.html

Liu, S. 2020. *Artificial Intelligence Funding United States 2011–2019.* Accessed on November 3, 2020. https://www.statista.com/statistics/672712/ai-funding-united-states/

Walch, K. 2020. *Why the Race for AI Dominance is More Global thank You Think.* Forbes Magazine, February 9, 2020. Accessed on November 3, 2020. https://www.forbes.com/sites/cognitiveworld/2020/02/09/why-the-race-for-ai-dominance-is-more-global-than-you-think/#7b273227121f

International Data Corporation. 2019. *Worldwide Spending on Artificial Intelligence Will Be Nearly $98 billion in 2023, According to IDC Spending Guide.* IDC. September 4, 2019. Accessed on November 3, 2020. https://www.idc.com/getdoc.jsp?containerId=prUS45481219

The United States of Artificial Intelligence Startups. Research Briefs, CBInsights. July 16, 2020. Accessed on November 3, 2020. https://www.cbinsights.com/research/artificial-intelligence-startup-us-map/

44. U.S. Department of Education, National Center for Education Statistics. 2020. *The Condition of Education 2020* (NCES 2020–144).

United States Census Bureau. 2019. *U.S. School Spending per Pupil Increased for Fifth consecutive Year, U.S.* Census Bureau Reports. May 21, 2019. Accessed on November 3, 2020. https://www.census.gov/newsroom/press-releases/2019/school-spending.html

45. Bandura, A. 2006. *Toward a Psychology of Human Agency.* Perspectives on Psychological Science, 1, 164–180.

Bandura, A. 2008. *The Reconstrual of "Free Will" from the Agentic Perspective of Social Cognitive Theory. In J. Baer, J. C. Kaufman & R. F. Baumeister (Eds.), Are We Free? Psychology and Free Will* (pp. 86–127). Oxford: Oxford University Press.

Bandura, A. 2017. *Toward a Psychology of Human Agency: Pathways and Reflections*. Perspectives on Psychological Science.

Bandura, A. 1989. *Human Agency in Social Cognitive Theory*. American Psychologist, 44, 1175–1184.

Bandura, A. 2006. *Growing Primacy of Human Agency in Adaptation and Change in the Electronic Era*. European Psychologist, 7, 2–16.

Bandura, A. 2001. *Social Cognitive Theory: An Agentic Perspective.* Annual review of psychology (Vol. 52, pp. 1–26). Palo Alto: Annual Reviews, Inc.

Bandura, A. 1982. *Self-Efficacy Mechanism in Human Agency*. American Psychologist, 37, 122–147.

CHAPTER 7

46. Sadie, S., ed. 1992. *The New Grove Dictionary of Opera*. London: Macmillan Reference.

    Solomon, M. 1995. *Mozart: A Life (1st ed.)* New York: HarperCollins.

47. Spaethling, R. 2005. *Mozart's Letters, Mozart's Life: Selected Letters*. New York: W.W. Norton & Co.

48. Solomon, M. 1995. *Mozart: A Life (1st ed.)* New York: HarperCollins.

49. Bandura, A. 2006. *Toward a Psychology of Human Agency*. Perspectives on Psychological Science. June 1, 2006.

    Fontan, J.; Twani, E. 2009. *The Unwakened Potential*. Sao Paulo: Anais EDUTEC.

50. Dweck, C. 2006. *Mindset: The New Psychology of Success*. New York, NY: Random House Publishing Group.

    Duckworth, A. 2016. *Grit, The Power of Passion and Perseverance.* New York: Simon & Schuster.

    Pink, D. 2009. *Drive: The Surprising Truth about What Motivates Us.* New York, NY: Riverhead Books.

    Aronica, L.; Robinson, K. 2009. *The Element: How Finding Your Passion Changes Everything.* London: Penguin Books.

    Duhigg, C. 2016. *Smarter, Faster, Better: The Secrets of Being Productive in Life and Business.* New York, NY: Random House.

51. Pink, D. 2009. *Drive: The Surprising Truth about What Motivates Us.* New York, NY: Riverhead Books.

52. Duhigg, C. 2016. *Smarter, Faster, Better: The Secrets of Being Productive in Life and Business.* New York, NY: Random House.

53. Bandura, A. 2006. *Toward a Psychology of Human Agency.* Perspectives on Psychological Science. June 1, 2006.

54. Dweck, C. 2006. *Mindset: The New Psychology of Success.* New York, NY: Random House Publishing Group.

    Duckworth, A. 2016. *Grit, The Power of Passion and Perseverance.* New York: Simon & Schuster.

    Bandura, A. 2006. *Toward a Psychology of Human Agency.* Perspectives on Psychological Science. June 1, 2006.

55. Landon, H. C. R. 1990. *1791: Mozart's Last Year.* London: Flamingo.

CHAPTER 8

56. Caldicott, S.; Gelb, M. 2008. *Innovate Like Edison—the success system of America's greatest inventor.* New York: Penguin Group.

57. Edison's Papers, June 19, 1884. Accessed on November 3, 2020. http://edison.rutgers.edu/NamesSearch/SingleDoc.php?DocId =D8429ZAO

CHAPTER 9

58. Fontan, J.; Twani, E. 2009. *The Unwakened Potential.* Sao Paulo: Anais EDUTEC.

    Fontan, J.; Twani, E. 2014. *A Glimpse of Fontan Relational Education.* Fort Lauderdale, FL. Accessed on November 3, 2020. https://www.learning1to1.net/articles.

59. diSessa, A. 2000. *Changing Minds: Computers, Learning, and Literacy.* Cambridge, MA: MIT Press.

    Linn, M.; His, S. 2000. *Computers, Teachers, Peers: Science Learning Partners.* Mahwah, NJ: Lawrence Erlbaum Associates.

60. Bruner, J. S.; Olver, R. R.; Greenfield, P. M.; et al. 1966. *Studies in Cognitive Growth.* New York: John Wiley & Sons.

61. Lea, S. J.; Stephenson, D.; Troy, J. 2003. *Higher Education Students' Attitudes to Student Centered Learning: Beyond 'educational bulimia.'* Studies in Higher Education 28(3), 321–334.

62. Ericsson A.; Pool R. 2016. *Peak: Secrets from the New Science of Expertise.* New York, NY: Mifflin Harcourt Publishing Company.

63. Gardner, H. 1993. *Multiple Intelligences: The Theory in Practice.* New York: Basic Books.

64. Bandura, A. 1997. *Self-efficacy: The Exercise of Self-Control.* New York: W.H. Freeman.

65. Bloom, B. 1984. *The 2 Sigma Problem: The Search for Methods of Group Instruction as Effective as One to One Tutoring.* Educational Researcher, 13(6), 4–16.

Ausubel, D. P.; Robinson, F. G. 1969. *School Learning: An Introduction to Educational Psychology.* New York: Holt, Rinehart & Winston.

Marzano, R.J. 2003. *What Works in Schools: Translating Research Into Action.* Alexandria, VA: ASCD.

66. Benson, P.; Voller, P. 1997. *Autonomy and Independence in Language Learning.* New York, NY: Routledge.

67. Ausubel, D.; Novak, J. D.; Hanesian, H. 1968. *Educational Psychology: A Cognitive View.* New York, NY: Holt, Rinehart and Winston.

68. Marzano, R. J.; Pickering, D. J.; Pollock, J. E. 2001.*Classroom instruction that works: Research-based strategies for increasing student achievement.* Alexandria, VA: Association for Supervision and Curriculum Development.

Beamish, J.; Trackman, T. 2019 *The Creative Brain.* New York, NY: New Balloon.

69. Fitts, P. M.; Posner, M. I. 1967. *Human performance.* Oxford: Brooks/Cole.

70. Chambliss, D. 1989. *The mundanity of Excellence: An Ethnographic Report on Stratification and Olympic Swimmers.* Hamilton College.

71. Dispenza, J. 2008. *Evolve Your Brain: The Science of Changing Your Mind.* Deerfield Beach, FL: Health Communications, Inc.

72. Latham, G.; Locke, E. 2002. *Building a Practically Useful Theory of Goal Setting and Task Motivation: A 35-Year Odyssey.* American Psychologist 57, no. 9 (2002): 705–717.

Milne, S.; Orbell, S.; Sheeran, P. 2002. *Combining Motivational and Volitional Interventions to Promote Exercise Participation: Protection Motivation Theory and Implementation Intentions.* British Journal of Health Psychology 7 (May 2002): 163–184.

Calderon, S.; Charney, D. S.; Cohen, H.; Feder, A.; Kim, J. J.; Mathé, A. A.; Wu, G. 2013. *Understanding Resilience.* Frontiers in Behavioral Science, February 15, 2013.

CHAPTER 10

73. Bandura, A. 2006. *Toward a Psychology of Human Agency.* Perspectives on Psychological Science. June 1, 2006.

Ericsson A.; Pool R. 2016. *Peak: Secrets From the New Science of Expertise.* New York, NY: Mifflin Harcourt Publishing Company.

CHAPTER 11

74. Bandura, A. 2006. *Toward a Psychology of Human Agency.* Perspectives on Psychological Science. June 1, 2006.

Pink, D. 2009. *Drive: The Surprising Truth about What Motivates Us.* New York, NY: Riverhead Books.

75. Learn About Concept Maps. IHMC. Accessed on November 3, 2020. http://cmap.ihmc.us/docs/learn.php.

CHAPTER 13

76. Albers, D. J.; Alexanderson, G. L.; Reid, C., eds. 1990. *George B. Dantzig. More Mathematical People.* San Diego, CA: Harcourt Brace Jovanovich.

77. Fast Facts: *Back to School Statistics.* National Center for Education Statistics. Accessed on November 3, 2020. https://nces.ed.gov/fastfacts/display.asp?id=372

78. Ocean Cleanup. Accessed on November 3, 2020. https://theoceancleanup.com/

79. Wamsley, L. 2017. *Troubled By Flint Water Crisis, 11-Year-Old Girl Invents Lead-Detecting Device.* October 20, 2017. Accessed on November 3, 2020. https://www.npr.org/sections/thetwo-way/2017/10/20/559071028/troubled-by-flint-water-crisis-11-year-old-girl-invents-lead-detecting-device

80. Cameron, C. 2015. *Kenyan teenager converts his school's poop into safe, clean energy.* Accessed on November 3, 2020. https://inhabitat.com/kenyan-student-converts-schools-waste-yes-poo-into-safe-clean-cooking-fuel/

81. Gilchrist, K. 2019. *The 10 Countries With the Fastest-Growing Earnings for Freelancers.* CNBC. August 6, 2019. Accessed on November 3, 2020. https://www.cnbc.com/2019/08/07/the-10-countries-with-the-fastest-growing-earnings-for-freelancers.html

    Ben. 2019. *Freelance Statistics: The Freelance Economy in Numbers.* FreeTrain. August 29, 2019. Accessed on November 3, 2020. https://benrmatthews.com/freelance-statistics/

82. Bandura, A. 1986. *Social Foundations of Thought and Action: A Social Cognitive Theory.* New Jersey: Prentice Hall.

    Bandura, A. 2006. *Toward a Psychology of Human Agency.* Perspectives on Psychological Science. June 1, 2006.

Made in United States
North Haven, CT
13 March 2022